"If you want to remain calm amidst the stress of modern life – this is the book you're looking for. A clear, practical and wonderfully approachable guide to something we all need more of these days… peace of mind."

TIMOTHY FREKE, best-selling author of *The Mystery Experience*

"Sandy has done it again. THUNK! awakens you to the realization that you have the power, right now, to be peaceful, and shows you how to have a much happier experience of being human."

NICK WILLIAMS, best-selling author of *Powerful Beyond Measure*

"Utterly life changing! Inspirational, but practical too."

SUZY GREAVES, best-selling author of *The Big Peace*

"Kick off your shoes, lie back, and enjoy this timely reminder that you have everything you need to experience bliss within you."

URSULA JAMES, best-selling author of *The Source*

"Thunk! shares a liberating way to break free from stress and find inner peace. Sandy gives you great insights and tools for creating deep transformations from the inside out."

JOSEPH CLOUGH, best-selling author of *Be Your Potential*

"If you want to shift your centre of gravity from stress to stillness, then this is the book to show you how."

DR. MARK ATKINSON, best-selling author of *True Happiness*

"I am genuine when I say that I think Thunk! is a masterpiece (or should I say master-peace!), for experienced meditators and beginners alike."

SASHA ALLENBY, best-selling author of *Matrix Reimprinting*

"Thunk! provides us with a breath-taking jaunt through the landscape of stilling conscious awareness. Using his reductionist approach Sandy encourages us to stop being Thunk! and gives us the very means to think precisely and economically, thereby creating peace in mind, body and soul. What a virtue!'"

STEWART PEARCE, best-selling author of *The Alchemy of Voice*

THUNK!

HOW TO **THINK LESS** FOR **SERENITY** AND **SUCCESS**

SANDY C. NEWBIGGING

FINDHORN PRESS

To Narain,
my first teacher of meditation.

You've taught me that I never
have to finish another thought in order
to enjoy the life I've always...

© Sandy C. Newbigging 2012

The right of Sandy C. Newbigging to be identified as the
author of this work has been asserted by him in accordance
with the Copyright, Designs and Patents Act 1998.

Published in 2012 by Findhorn Press, Scotland

ISBN 978-1-84409-603-9

Edited by Jacqui Lewis
Cover design by Richard Crookes
Interior design by Damian Keenan
Printed and bound in the EU

1 2 3 4 5 6 7 8 9 17 16 15 14 13 12

Published by
Findhorn Press
117-121 High Street,
Forres IV36 1AB,
Scotland, UK

t +44 (0)1309 690582
f +44 (0)131 777 2711
e info@findhornpress.com
www.findhornpress.com

Contents

*"Tension is who
you think you should be.
Relaxation is who
you are."*

CHINESE PROVERB

Are You Being Thunk?

· · · ·

IF YOU CANNOT STOP THINKING WHENEVER YOU WANT, THEN YOU ARE BEING THUNK!

LET'S GET SOMETHING CLEAR FROM THE START. I'm not saying your mind is bad and you should never think again. Your mind is a remarkable tool that you can use to create marvellous things. However, what's become very apparent to me is that most people I meet don't know how to *not* think. And that certainly *is* a problem. Thinking too much is very stressful, leads to ill-health, inhibits creativity, postpones your peace, limits your love, and, perhaps most importantly, prevents you from knowing the unbounded brilliance of your real self.

You are not alone if you find it hard to not think!

Most people I meet from around the world at my clinics, courses and retreats find it near impossible to stop their minds from working overtime. They think all day long, and some of them even think their way through the night too. Unable to reduce the deluge of thoughts occurring, their unhealthy habit of thinking has become insistent, uncontrollable and intense.

Mind mastery is attained when you can use your mind instead of your mind using you.

If you cannot switch off and stop thinking at will, then your relationship with your mind has become unbalanced and unproductive. Rather than you using your mind as the magnificent tool that it is, and then putting it down when you're done, your mind is quite literally *using* you! I would suggest that the result of this incessant thinking is that you aren't actually thinking any more, but instead, you are *being thunk*!

> *Thunking occurs when you cannot stop engaging in and reacting to the train of thoughts passing through your mind.*

Being **THUNK** is one of the biggest problems on the planet today. It is a hidden cause of conflict, suffering and stress and is the main reason why you are not experiencing the peace and productivity that you are inherently capable of. If you are being **THUNK** then you are unwittingly giving the content of your thoughts the unwarranted power to negatively impact your moods, health, relationships, peace and prosperity. Worst of all, it is an utterly unnecessary problem because re-addressing your relationship with your mind is possible for everyone I have met.

> *People think all the time because they don't know of a better way to relate to their mind.*

Before I learnt about the benefits of not thinking, I focused my personal-development efforts on changing my negative thoughts and emotions. Despite great efforts to improve the content of my mind, I found that I still got stressed and my moods continued to go up and down. Why? Because I had not solved the underlying cause of my problems: namely, my habit of thinking.

Thankfully, I've now discovered that cultivating a more consistent sense of contentment, inner peace and happiness is less about *changing your mind,* and much more about *changing your relationship with your mind.* By doing the latter, you are able to enjoy more inner peace and productivity, irrespective of what thoughts are happening in your mind. Imagine that!

> *You never have to be a victim of the content of your thoughts ever again.*

Waking up to such a liberating possibility is one of the most important things you can ever do. As a result, this book is about showing you how to shift your focus from the *content* of your ever-changing mind to the permanently peaceful *context* of your mind. By helping you to let go of your temporary thoughts and emotions, my hope is that you will rediscover your real self – which is present, powerful and peaceful.

By learning to think less and resting in your real self, I want you to enjoy the most amazing life, free from mind-based problems and full of love, health, wealth and happiness.

To your freedom,

Sandy C. Newbigging

Who Would Have Thunk It?

· · · ·

BEING PEACEFUL AND PRODUCTIVE IS POSSIBLE!

THE TRUTH IS THE TRUTH – THERE'S ONLY ONE AND IT'S INEFFABLE.
The ways of describing it are myriad, though all have one thing in common: the power of metaphor. Metaphor is how we point to the way. When someone's metaphor resonates with you, even or especially if it's different from your own, it helps not only to stretch your mind but also to reinforce your own way by reminding you of what you already know, but might have forgotten in the rush.

When I met Sandy, I was instantly struck by his enthusiastic approach to spreading his word, and his courage in dedicating himself to forging a fresh path. I recognized myself in him, and was deeply touched by the quality of his soul.

In this magnificent new book of his, through his innovative metaphor, alluding to the same truth and path I point to myself in all my work, he does so in a totally unique, original way. So that although I've written fourteen books on the same topic, which normally leaves me nonplussed by offerings in a similar vein, I have been highly inspired reading this one and feel privileged to be writing the foreword.

As he so eruditely observes, inner peace and the joy deriving thereof is brought about not so much by changing your thinking as some would have us believe, but by shifting the whole process of thinking itself, namely by entering the meditation state, whence pure awareness arises.

Pure awareness, uncluttered by thoughts of how well or badly you're doing in the game of local life, untroubled by the usual internal commentary and debate, facilitates the emptiness, hence receptivity espoused in the Taoist tradition I live by and teach myself. Being empty and in a peaceful state, they say, even gods and spirits are drawn to you bearing great gifts, let alone mere mortals.

In other words, seek peace and all else will be added. In **THUNK!** Sandy shows you how in the most splendidly eloquent way, and I've no doubt you'll enjoy and benefit from each and every word.

BAREFOOT DOCTOR,
Best-Selling Author

"There is nothing either good or bad, but thinking makes it so."

WILLIAM SHAKESPEARE

To Think or Not to Think?

• • • •

THAT IS THE LIFE-CHANGING QUESTION!

LEARNING TO THINK LESS CAN REAP RAPID REWARDS. Instead of having to individually change all of your negative thoughts and emotions so that you can *eventually* enjoy some peace, you can *immediately* connect with a presence of peace that exists within you right now.

Take a moment to consider the implications of this remarkable possibility. You don't need to spend days, weeks or years trying to fix, change and improve the content of your mind so that *one day* you can enjoy a sense of serenity. Rather, enjoying your birthright can be as simple and immediate as tapping into an inner stillness that is *already* present.

Healing your relationship with your mind reconnects you with ever-increasing levels of peace, happiness, love, joy and contentment. It can once and for all free you from limited thinking and enable you to enjoy the abundance that life has to offer. What's more, you can rediscover the unbounded brilliance of what I call your real self – the still, silent, spacious, conscious awareness that exists beyond the confines of your mind.

From being your real self as you go about your day, you can experience life in its perfection, free from problems, while resting within an inner reservoir of perfect peace, for life.

But I'm getting ahead of myself. Let me begin by sharing a bit about how my life twisted and turned and went up and down in such a way that I got to a point where I was sick and tired of thinking so much…

Everything Was Going Great

I was achieving my goals, and was living what I thought was a successful life. But then, out of the blue reality hit me. Despite my life being exactly how I'd always wanted it to be, I realized I wasn't happy yet, I didn't feel successful, nor was I experiencing much peace of mind.

Reality Check

As the creator of a powerful form of therapy called the Mind Detox Method, working internationally with people at my clinics, courses and retreats, I was surprised to realize that irrespective of all the work I'd done to change my own mind, I continued to occasionally experience negative thoughts and emotions. What made matters worse was noticing that my therapy clients were having the same experience. Don't get me wrong, the Mind Detox Method is an incredibly effective way of healing physical conditions, clearing emotional baggage and improving a person's life. But despite this, I noticed that my clients and I were not experiencing permanent peace of mind yet.

My Rock Bottom Wake-Up Call

Feeling frustrated, I realized that I could no longer rely on my future to fulfil me. I knew continuing to work so hard to accomplish bigger and better goals wasn't going to relieve my eternal itch that *there must be more to life than this*.

To make matters worse, my increasing frustration led to a rocky time in my relationship, which inevitably ended with my partner leaving, along with the beautiful child I'd been raising, the great house I was living in, the fancy car I was driving and the pile of money we'd jointly secured as projects fell away.

Rock bottom, needing peace, I started exploring alternative ways of thinking, being and living. It was around about that time that I met a group of meditation teachers who changed my life. I saw in their eyes a peace and joy that I had never seen before; and the more time I spent with them the more obvious it became to me that their inner peace was very consistent. Hungry to experience the same, I packed my bag again and headed off to meditate with them for a few months. I spent ten weeks on the island of Patmos in Greece, followed by a further fourteen weeks in the mountains of Mexico.

A Total Turnaround In Thinking

I discovered that the real cause of my persistent problems had never been my failings at 'thinking positively'. Instead, my habit of think-ing was *in itself* the ultimate cause of my problems. When I was thinking I was missing the peace that's always present. And as I learnt to think less and be present, my life became much more enjoy-able. Since being shown this enlightening truth, I've experienced levels of peace, happiness, love and contentment beyond what I ever thought possible. With this book I hope to help you do the same.

Freedom From Thinking Too Much

Ultimately, when it comes to you enjoying lifelong inner peace and prosperity it's how you relate to your mind that matters. If you have to stop your negative thoughts to be at peace or feel abundant, then you will remain a victim of the random movement of your mind for ever. However, the moment you become aware of the still, silent context of your mind, you notice there is instantly more calm and fullness than there was a moment ago. What's more, resting aware of this still silence gives you the power to choose a life lived in a state of unconditional happiness and constant contentment. Amid an ocean of what can be best described as pure, deep and unbounded love.

Sound good? Well, the best news of all is that it is possible for you. Yes, that's right, YOU!!!

Irrespective of what's happened during your life and who you think you are today, what you consider to be your successes and failures, good attributes and bad bits, your good deeds and downright awful ones and your ups and downs. Whether you have the body, looks, love life, education, career, money, home, hobbies or life you think you should. I'm here to tell you one indisputable truth.

None of these things ultimately matter. Not one iota. Not when it comes to you having the same ability as anyone else to experience serenity and success now. Yes you read that right; there are no prerequisites, no rites of passage and nothing about you needs to change or improve for you to enjoy peace for life. You see, the truth is that whether you believe it or not, you are *already* an absolutely amazing, infinitely conscious, utterly gorgeous, perfectly peaceful, love-filled human being. This is *what you are*. Whether you like it or not! All these wonderful things come built in; your gift for being born. And it's your birthright to experience the *truth of what you are*.

You may not believe it. You may not feel it. It may not be your current experience. The truth is it doesn't stop it being true! Truth overrules beliefs and feelings. Truth is absolutely real and permanent. Beliefs and feelings are only relatively real and temporary. And the truth is *you are* all these wonderful things I've described, and more.

On offer here is everything you could possibly hope for. You have the opportunity of resting in the heart of all that is good. Simply by no longer buying into illusionary thinking about what you're not, you can discover the pristine peace and unbounded beauty of *what you've been* the entire time.

Peace Is Your Most Natural Way To Be

Not being peaceful actually takes effort and causes the body stress. The mind is the master and the body is the servant; or, put another way, the body follows the mind. Leading scientists have found stress to be one of the main causes of physical illnesses and conditions and, conversely, the body heals more quickly and functions optimally when it is resting, or in other words, at peace.

You were <u>not</u> put on this planet to get sick.
You were born to live.

You were born to live a breathtakingly awe-inspiring life! You have the potential and opportunity to both feel fantastic and manifest a magnificent reality. Your most natural way of being is to experience perfect peace, limitless love, heaps of happiness and total completeness, without needing any specific reasons to do so. We are taught we need to *do* things to *be* all these great things. This simply is not true. The reality is quite the opposite. Simply resting back into what I refer to as your real self, you can get everything you could possibly want.

This isn't optimistic. It is simply your birthright.

Isn't it a relief to recognize truth? Your heart knows this to be true. It responds to these words. Let that inner knowing be your guide. Trust your heart. Question your head. Because what you are going to discover is that peace is available to you now; by learning to think less, be present, and explore what exists beyond the confines of your mind.

The Peace That's Always Present

Within your awareness, right now, is the ongoing existence of a still, silent space. A peace. However, it is possible to miss it because you've forgotten it's there.

Growing up, you were encouraged to put 100 per cent of your attention on the movement of your mind, your body and your life. You were rarely, if ever, educated in the enlightening truth that absolutely everything happens within a constant context of pure and perfect, still silent awareness. In other words, that your mind, your body and your world all exist within an infinite and ongoing presence of peace.

So you can end up missing the peace that is your birthright to enjoy. You feel what you focus on. So by putting your attention on things in your awareness that constantly move, are forever changing and, by their very nature, are in a constant state of flux, you end up feeling uneasy. Not only that, but because you end up missing a huge piece of yourself and reality, you can end up living with a sense that something is missing; that there must be more to life than what you are currently experiencing. Can you relate to this?

Closer Than Your Next Breath

The peace you seek is always present. It exists only now. However, because you've been taught to think about the past and future you can end up, in your mind, one step removed from the peace that's present. The good news is that the peace you seek is right under your nose. Closer than your next breath. It is you. It is here. And irrespective of how long you may have been distracted from it, it only takes an instant to return home.

My primary message to you within this book is this:

> *Put your attention back on the still silent space that re-sides within your conscious awareness right now and you will instantly reconnect with the pristine peace that is always present.*

The path of peace is through a silent doorway of stillness. By bringing your attention back to the stillness that exists, always now, you immediately rest in the unbounded beauty and peaceful presence that is your real self.

Today you embark on a journey of freedom from thinking too much, which has been known for a very long time as many things, including the Path of the Sages, the Path of Return, the Path of the Hero and the Path of Joy. It is all these things and more. What you are going to learn is simple, but please don't underestimate its importance and magnitude. Knowing your real self is the purpose for which you were born.

ABOUT THIS BOOK

THUNK! is about much less being infinitely more. It is intended to be a small book that gives you enough guidance to get what's on offer, but without going into too much detail so that you get lost in the content. Simplicity is key, so please avoid over-complicating things; if while you're reading, it ever feels difficult, then stop and take a timeout. The very act of trying to 'get it' can keep you stuck in the habit of thinking.

Thinking less is much easier than you may think –
so keep it simple.

THUNK! is about gently disengaging your grasp on the mind, rather than going to any great efforts to manipulate, change or fix it. It's about learning how to rest aware of the present moment occurring, and noticing what exists when you let go of thinking.

Being you has to be easy, natural and simple.

As you are rediscovering an aspect to you that *already* exists, at some level you know much of what you are going to read. The purpose of the following pages is to help you remember what you inherently know and encourage you to play with the games provided. Doing so will redirect your attention back to the here and now – where you will naturally find your real self to be. Despite it being easy, please take heed of the following tips for getting the most from this book.

TIP #1 **Be Innocent**
The chances are you've read other self-help books and this isn't your very first attempt at wanting to enjoy more peace of mind and happiness. Most people who use my methods have tried other approaches

and been let down. However, irrespective of what's happened in the past, you need to leave the past where it belongs – in the past!

I encourage you to trust the process, suspend judgement and jump in with as much childlike curiosity and innocence as you can muster. Your mind, body and universe respond quickest to you being one-pointed by taking action without tentativeness. Leave doubt at the door when using the methods outlined in this book and do your best to not let scepticism steal your success.

TIP #2 Be Willing to Change

Although, in reality, most people's comfort zones are pretty uncomfortable, thinking your way through your day can become a familiar habit. Be completely honest with yourself when considering these questions: *Are you willing to draw a line in the sand and step out into perhaps unfamiliar territory? Are you willing to do things differently? Are you willing to trust the process even if, at the start, some parts may seem pointless? And are you willing to do whatever it takes to build momentum towards new, healthier habits?*

If yes, then great! You are reading the right book.

TIP #3 Be Easy on Yourself

Reading a book like this can make you aware of how your thoughts, emotions and lifestyle may be negatively impacting on health, wealth and happiness. But what's very important to keep in mind is that although your mind, emotions and life *are* your responsibility, you have not intentionally *done it to yourself* and it is not your fault. The ultimate cause of your problems has been your habit of thinking, and you haven't necessarily had guidance or support to live in any other way. Blaming yourself or feeling guilty about how you've been does not help you heal – quite the opposite in fact. Be easy on yourself and gently make whatever positive changes you can.

TIP #4 Be Committed

Do you really want to experience life differently? Are you willing to persist until you get the results you want?

People who have changed their relationship with their mind have made it their number one priority, for as long as it has taken. I didn't do it in a day and I continue to practise the techniques shared within this book. Instead of looking for a magic pill to magically fix everything, I encourage you to make the most of your journey by being gently persistent.

TIP #5 Finish the Book!

You bought this book because you want to stop thinking so much. It can help you get what you want, but you must commit to reading the entire book. Thinking is a lifelong habit, so it is wise to equip yourself with the right intellectual know-how to make the shift. To stop halfway would be to be within a hair's breadth of enjoying the most wonderful life, but then turn away at the last moment. Read to the very end of the book and set the intention to consistently and actively apply the exercises shared. I want you to discover the inner peace that is always present.

If you are ready for a new way of relating to your mind, can follow instructions and remain open-minded throughout, then I have complete confidence in you. Within this book is ancient wisdom with a modern twist for enjoying the unbounded benefits that can come from partaking in the liberating adventure of freeing yourself from thinking too much.

"Unless you become like children,
you will never enter
the Kingdom of Heaven.
Whoever humbles himself like a child
is the greatest."

MATTHEW 18 : 3-4

CHAPTER ONE

Letting Go of What You Know

• • • •

UN-LEARNING TO BE INNOCENT AGAIN

INNOCENCE IS BLISS! When I asked my spiritual teacher to guide me towards freedom from thinking too much, he responded with the most important question I'd ever been asked. He compassionately challenged me: "Are you willing to let go of everything you think you know in order to be free?" In that moment he helped me to see that all the knowledge I'd gathered from countless books and courses had not brought me peace. On the contrary – in some ways I was more stressed and confused than ever!

Before being asked this question, I had assumed that the answer to my heart's yearning for peace was going to be found by finding *the lost secret* that had somehow eluded me my entire life; an enlightening piece of information that, when I read or heard it, would, as if by magic, make everything make sense and catapult me into nirvana. So I'd been searching high and low, reading ancient and modern texts from far and wide and asking every clever person who would listen, waiting and hoping that one day the missing piece of my peace-of-mind puzzle would finally fall into place. But that 'aha' moment had never come and my quiet frustration had only grown into an inner ache that I carried with me everywhere

I went. So when I was invited to let go of everything I thought I knew, I was ripe to revel in such a delightful possibility. Could it be true that all of my concepts and ideas *about* how peace can be experienced were the very thing standing in my way to experiencing it now?

What if, perhaps ironically, letting go of what I knew by returning to innocence, I could finally experience first-hand the peace-filled liberation that I'd been learning *about* for so long?

Be Like Children

Ever looked into the eyes of a baby? It's lovely, isn't it? One of the reasons why you enjoy it so much is that you recognize something. Something you've known but perhaps forgotten. What you see is undiluted consciousness aware of the present moment. The baby's mind is empty. It has no beliefs. It isn't judging. It isn't thinking to itself, "Jeez, she needs to get her roots redone!" or, "Wow, he's put on a few kilos". Nope, nothing like that. It's not thinking. Instead, it is just observing.

Innocent, with absolutely zero expectations, it is fully experiencing whatever it is aware of right now. Fully connected to unbounded awareness, it holds nothing and is completely open to whatever happens next. And because the baby hasn't yet learnt beliefs about how life *should* look, it is able to be open and fully experience the fullness of each moment.

Learning To Be Innocent Again

For you to get what's on offer here, you need to see beyond your conditioned mind by being completely innocent with me now. Leave any opinions, ideas and past experiences at the door. There is no place for them in this entirely new moment.

Explore what it is like to bring nothing into this moment with you. Start to innocently observe what's happening now as if you don't know what's going to happen next. Because in reality you don't know what's going to happen. You just *think* you do. And thinking stops you from directly experiencing what is *actually* happening in reality. Thinking acts as a veil that stands between what you think you are and the true wonders of what you really are and what life is.

There is a world of difference between knowing about peace and actually experiencing peace.

Play with having no preconceived ideas about how peace of mind is achieved. Knowledge knows *about* what you want, but where you're headed is the *direct experience* of what you want. Get the difference? Would you prefer to know about your favorite food or do you want to taste it? Do you want to know about the present moment or do you want to *be* present? Do you want to know about peace or do you want to experience it?

You could have memorized an entire library of books about peace, but still not be *experiencing* peace. (Trust me, I tried!) Knowledge can only take you so far. There is always a point where you must be willing to let go of what you *think you know* in order to actually experience.

Trust that nothing in the past is worth thinking about and nothing in the future could possibly be any better than what you are experiencing right now. Be with me now as if you don't know anything of value to help you to experience this moment any better. Let go of expectations of how things should be. Let go of the notion that you know how life works. Free yourself from future expectations. They only dull your experience of the magnificent moment you're in.

Innocence is fresh. It is utterly open, holds nothing and is completely empty. If you are full of concepts and ideas about life then there is no space for you to experience truth. And the truth is that the kingdom of heaven, whatever your personal idea of what that is, is at hand. You arrived the day you were born, and you were born with peace, love and joy built in, but have been led to believe you have to wait until things are different before you can experience what is actually your birthright to enjoy right now. Letting go of what you think you know helps you to step beyond the concepts of the mind to directly experience the truth and peace that is already present.

Remember the innocent baby whose mind is empty of judgments, beliefs and expectation? Over the next few days you are going to explore and play with what it is like to be innocent again.

GAME #1

Fresh Eyes

Explore what it is like to be completely fresh and innocent with the people in your life. See them with fresh eyes. Let go of any preconceived ideas you may have about your partner, parent(s), family members and friends, colleagues and even strangers. Just be with them fully, giving them your 100 per cent attention, as if this is the first and last time you will get to be in their company. Don't try to manipulate your interactions to gain any specific outcome. Instead, be open to whatever naturally wants to occur. Pretend there is no past and you have no history with anyone. Pretend the people in your life are perfect exactly as they are. That they just want to be happy, experience peace and know they are loved. Your 'soul task' is to interact with other people with no expectations. Just be open and curious as to what might happen. Look with fresh eyes and notice how much better life becomes.

GAME #2

Making The Mundane Magical

Play with what it is like to be completely fresh and innocent with any mundane tasks that you do over the next few days: doing the dishes, the daily commute to work, having a shower, putting your make-up on, tying your tie etc. Pretend these activities are your favourite pastimes and give them your full attention. You are playing with forgetting that something is boring, a person is difficult or anything should happen in any particular way. You are letting go of the notion that you think you've figured out this thing called Life. Be innocent like a child, curious and open to whatever happens.

*"Only when you give up
your attraction to thinking
do you realize that it takes
a massive amount of energy and
effort to engage in thinking."*

MKI

CHAPTER TWO

Beyond Conventional Thinking

. . . .

CHANGE HOW YOU RELATE TO YOUR THOUGHTS

PEACE IS POSSIBLE WITHOUT HAVING TO STILL YOUR MIND. How many thoughts pass through your mind on a daily basis? Incredibly, it has been said that the average person has around 100,000 thoughts every day – or approximately one thought every second. That's a lot of thoughts! Perhaps more worrying, though, is the number of these thoughts that are negative and are thus having a potentially harmful impact on your body, your mood and your life.

Having observed the content of my own mind during countless hours of meditation and listened to literally hundreds of other people's minds when doing Mind Detox, I believe it would be very fair to suggest that at least half of the average person's thinking is negative. Does that percentage sound reasonable to you? It certainly did to me, at least until I realized that 50 per cent worked out at a massive 50,000 negative thoughts a day! This obviously makes any attempts to think only positive thoughts a monumental task.

The Myth Of Positive Thinking

Now I'm a believer in, and promoter of, the benefits of being positive. However, the sheer quantity of thoughts makes any attempts to change your mind so that you *only* have 'positive thoughts' an almost impossible task. So if you've done your best to think positive, but not mastered it, be easy on yourself. Such a quest is made even trickier by the fact that most of your thoughts pass through your mind without you having any control over them whatsoever. So is it a lost cause? No!

A Very Appealing Solution Indeed

Rather than attempt the impractical task of changing the thousands of negative thoughts that may pass through your mind on a daily basis, I recommend that instead you do one thing: change your *relationship* with the thousands of thoughts. The goal: to experience an ongoing sense of serenity and success, irrespective of the kinds of thoughts that pass through your mind in any given moment.

Change Your Relationship With Your Mind

Most people I meet spend their days jumping from thought to thought and, as a direct consequence, experiencing a rollercoaster of emotions. Much of their stress is the direct result of them being completely focused on the *content* of their mind rather than the *context* in which the movement of their mind happens. They are focused on their thoughts, rather than the vast silent stillness in which their thoughts take place.

Imagine you are outside on a clear sunny day, looking up at the sky. Then, out of the blue, a bird flies across your field of vision. Without realizing, you take your attention away from the vast sky and follow the flight of the bird. The same happens in your awareness every day. Thoughts are something you are aware of. Thoughts are movement in your mind, yet they all happen within the context of still, silent, spacious awareness. By learning to let your attention rest on the stillness, rather than on the constant movement, you can experience a peace far beyond what you ever thought possible.

Peace Of Mind With A Million Thoughts

Until you become the master of your mind, your mind is the master of you. You will find yourself feeling up and down like a yo-yo depending on the quality of thoughts passing through your mind. If your mind produces happy thoughts you feel happy. If sad thoughts pass through then you feel sad. If confident thoughts happen you stand tall, but if fearful thoughts flood in, you can want to run scared. Thoughts happen, but if you are 100 per cent engaged in the movement of your mind then you will react like a puppet on strings. The good news is that it doesn't have to be this way.

> *Your peace need not be dependent upon the quality of your thoughts.*

Changing your relationship with your mind makes it possible for you to have negative thoughts without them affecting your peace in the slightest. Imagine that: your mind doesn't need to affect your peace any longer. On the contrary, by cultivating the ability to selectively choose which thoughts you engage in, you can use your mind to help you to create the success you want – instead of your mind negatively using you.

Your mind can become like a radio on in the background; you can tune in to the songs you enjoy (the thoughts that are useful to you), and tune out the bad news (the downward spiralling thoughts that lead to stress, suffering and separation). You can go through your day resting in peace, free. Even better news: you already possess an important skill to be able to do what I'm suggesting.

Have you ever been out with a friend at a busy bar or restaurant where, despite the noise, you've been able to ignore the people talking right beside you by focusing your attention on your friend's voice? (Or maybe the stranger beside you was having a more interesting conversation than your friend and you ended up tuning out your friend to listen to the other person?!). In both of these scenarios you have directed your attention to where you wanted it. The same skill is required for enjoying peace with a mind full of thoughts.

Ultimately, when it comes to enjoying inner peace, it's how you relate to your mind that matters. The moment you become aware of and place your attention upon what I will refer in this book as your real self – the still, conscious awareness that is silently aware of whatever is happening right now – you will find that there is instantly more peace than there was a moment earlier. What's more, you will then have the power to cultivate a life lived in a state of pristine peace, boundless bliss and constant contentment, amid a sea of what can be best described as pure, deep and limitless love. Sound good?

Let's get started in helping you to change your relationship with your thoughts.

You Are Not Your Thoughts

Peace of mind is possible while having thoughts because you are not your thoughts. Remember, thousands of thoughts pass through your awareness every day. They are constantly coming and going; that's what thoughts do. Thoughts appear for only a moment and then disappear to be replaced with another thought and then another one.

You exist even when you are not having thoughts.

Yet, despite countless thoughts coming and going today, there has been an aspect to you that has been here the entire time. An aspect to you that is permanent. That's your real self. It is continually present, irrespective of the quality or quantity of thoughts that come and go. This undeniable fact means one very important truth: You have thoughts but you are not your thoughts.

LET'S PLAY A GAME

Counting Thoughts

But don't take my word for it. Stop reading, close your eyes and watch your mind; quietly observe the thoughts flowing through your mind. Then, whenever you become aware of a thought – which could be about this topic, something you need to do later, or anything else – simply give the thought a number: one, two, three and so on. Awareness of a sound occurring is a thought. Awareness of a physical sensation is a thought. Even the voice in your head saying you aren't having any thoughts is a thought! So make sure you count them all. How many thoughts can you count over the next two minutes?

Stop Reading And Do It Now

Having done that, how many thoughts did you count: two, twenty-two, 202? It really doesn't matter how many. What matters is the fact that you could count even one thought. Why? Because this shows that you cannot *be* your thoughts. Instead, you are that which is aware of your thoughts. A thought is an object and you are the observer of the object. One is constant, whereas the other is constantly changing. Thoughts come and go. But *you* don't.

You are that which is aware of your thoughts, but you are not your thoughts! What a relief.

TOP TIP **Thinking About VS Directly Experiencing**

There is a huge difference between thinking about this game and actually doing it, now. If you do it immediately, then it will work for you – it has for 100 per cent of the people I've used it with! However, if you think about doing it, then you will end up in your head, one step removed from the direct experience of what it is I'm showing you.

The same goes for everything else I talk about in this book. It is very easy to unwittingly slip into your mind and start evaluating and judging what's being said, rather than going beyond the confines of your mind to directly experience what I'm saying. So if any of the games don't work for you, check in to see if, in that moment, you are actually doing them, or just thinking about doing them. There's a massive difference between thinking and experiencing and your peace is dependent upon you knowing the difference.

Stop Giving Away Power To Your Thoughts

No thought has the inherent power to negatively affect your mood or life success. The only way you can give thoughts power is by identifying with them through the unconscious act of thinking. To help you get your head around this, let me share an amazing analogy taught to me by my spiritual teacher.

Imagine you are outdoors with your best friend on a nice sunny day, sitting at the side of a busy road. You have been given the simple task of counting all the red cars that drive by. As you relax at the side of the road, a few cars come by – one blue, another black and then a red one, which you count. A little more time passes and more cars drive by. You continue to sit safely at the side of the road, feeling quite serene and happy as you enjoy the scene.

Then, as a red car comes by, your friend jumps up, runs after it and, with a spectacular leap, manages to grab the car's rear bumper, at which point they start being dragged up the road. You can see very clearly that they are getting hurt and are confused as to why they are holding on so tight. So you shout after your friend – "Let go!" – to which they shout back that the red car is hurting them. You shout back "The car isn't hurting you; you are getting hurt because you are holding on to it. Let go! Let go!" The same is true for your thoughts.

Thoughts have no power to hurt you or hold you back from being a success in life. What hurts and limits you is holding onto them through the act of thinking. As you learn to change your relationship with your mind you can learn to let go of your thoughts, so that they lose their power to negatively impact on your life, for good.

TOP TIP The Voice In Your Head Is A Thought Too

You have a voice in your head that sounds like you. It commentates on everything that happens, impacts on how you feel and even talks about the thoughts that are happening in your mind. When learning to relate to your mind in a more neutral manner, it helps massively to understand that it is not so much your thoughts that cause stress, but more the mental commentary *about* your thoughts.

Thoughts are neutral. It is your commentator that judges them as either positive or negative. So as you embark on thinking less, make sure you aim to be less governed by the voice in your head too. It is a thought like all the rest and by *seeing* the voice instead of *being* the voice, life becomes more serene.

Let's Make Sure We Are On The Same Page

There is an aspect to you that is permanent, but you also have thoughts that are temporary. The purpose of this chapter has been to introduce you to the possibility that you can change your relationship with your mind so that your thoughts can exist without them impacting on your peace and prosperity. This is possible because, as discussed earlier, you are not your thoughts. Instead, you are that which is aware of your thoughts – and that awareness is beyond the mind and already serene.

> *The sky doesn't care how many birds fly through it. Neither does it care if they are white doves or blackbirds. The same is true for your conscious awareness.*

By becoming aware, you experience what your own awareness is like. Which is, yes you guessed it, peaceful. Much serenity and success comes from you learning how to put most of your attention on your conscious awareness, rather than being solely focused on what you are aware of. By making this shift in where you put your attention, you reconnect with the aspect of your real self that is permanently peaceful.

"You are never upset for the reason your mind tells you."

MKI

CHAPTER THREE

Freedom From Feeling Bad

• • • •

CHANGE HOW YOU RELATE TO YOUR EMOTIONS

PEACE IS POSSIBLE WITHOUT HAVING TO GET RID OF YOUR EMOTIONS. Emotions come and go, but your real self does not. The chances are you've experienced a range of emotions during the past few hours. Similar to thoughts, emotions happen, but only for a while before they move on to be replaced by some other emotion. I appreciate that some emotions appear to be more comfortable than others, but what's more important to recognize when it comes to experiencing more serenity and success is the fact that emotions are temporary. And there is an aspect to you that is permanently in existence, throughout each and every day. Yes, you have emotions, but you are not your emotions.

Because of this, it is possible to change your relationship with your emotions to the extent that you can be at peace with how you are feeling.

> *"Before I was enlightened I was depressed.*
> *After I was enlightened I was depressed,*
> *but I didn't care anymore!"*
> ANTHONY DE MELLO [1]

Emotional Liberation

Emotions only become problematic if you start thinking about them in a way that causes you to resist their existence. Thinking about your emotions often leads to mental analysis as your mind tries to figure out why they are happening and what you can do to make them go away. But the truth is, your emotions don't need to go away for you to enjoy more peace.

Peace is not the absence of emotions.

Relating to your emotions from a more neutral perspective leads to immense freedom. The trick is to learn how to be at peace with how you are feeling. And the good news is: peace comes built in; so, rather than spending years trying to fix, change and improve your emotions individually so that you eventually enjoy peace, you can connect with inner peace right now. Wow!

Even better, when you relate to all of your emotions in a more positive way, all feelings can become an exquisite and enlivening experience.

Stop working towards peace and, instead, start walking the path of peace.

Freely Flowing Emotions

Emotions are in effect 'energy in *motion*' within your body–mind. They are designed to flow and go without obstruction, very much like the weather. However, it is possible for them to become stuck. Emotions labelled by the mind as negative, such as anger, sadness, fear, guilt, hurt and grief, are the most common emotions to become stuck because most people are conditioned to resist feeling them. I've observed that if emotions remain trapped, over time they can become harmful for the body.

> *By changing your relationship with your emotions you reduce the stressful load on your body–mind and benefit from enhanced energy levels.*

Two Questions That Make Emotions Stuck

Whenever you experience emotions it is common for your mind to automatically ask two questions: *What am I feeling* and *why am I feeling this way?* You may not be aware of these questions being asked, but if you ever struggle with your emotions then you can be sure that they are happening. Your mind attaches labels to the energy generated as feelings occur, and tells stories to try to explain why they are occurring; thus these two questions slow down the natural flow of your emotions.

No Negative Or Positive Emotions

Duality is a mind-made illusion; or, in other words, there are no positive or negative emotions, only energy. It is just your mind that labels different energetic experiences as either good or bad. Based on these labels, which include 'happiness', 'sadness', 'fear', 'excitement' and many more, your mind then deems the energy positive or negative, right or wrong. If your mind decides that the energy is negative, you often end up resisting the feeling. However, as the well-known phrase goes: 'What you resist persists.' Resistance ends up putting much attention on the very feeling your mind has decided you don't want; and this attention, in and of itself, can cause the emotion to stick around longer than necessary.

Let's explore this further by checking out the negative emotions in the boxes below:

Anger	Sadness	Fear
Anxiety	Guilt	Panic

These are the common labels used for different emotional experiences. However, what's important to realize is that all of these labels are learnt. Growing up, whenever you experienced emotions, the people around you told you what you were feeling. They might say, for example, 'Don't be sad', so over time you learnt that a) this energy was called 'sadness' and b) you shouldn't experience it. Over the years you have picked up lots of labels for the energy occurring within your body–mind, and decided which energies were positive and which were negative.

But who says there are multiple energies? What if there is only one energy occurring within you?

One Energy

The Ebb And Flow Of Energy Intensity

Take away the mind-made boxes that are causing the appearance of separate emotions and what's left is what I call a 'one energy'. Ultimately, there is only this one energy within your body–mind; the appearance that there are a number of different emotions is created by the intensity of the one energy fluctuating. Low intensity is often labelled as 'sadness' whereas high-energy intensity ends up being branded as 'fear', 'anxiety' or 'excitement'. Letting go of these individual labels attached to your emotions, and instead relating to your emotions as a one energy that varies in intensity, will help you to feel more at peace with however you happen to be feeling.

> *It has been said that there is only Love. What if all of your feelings are actually fragrances of Love? Would you resist the energy or simply let it be?*

Believing The Story Causes Suffering

In my opinion, it is the second question about feelings that has the greatest impact on your emotional well-being and whether, during your daily life, you experience serenity or stress.

Your mind has an amazing ability to come up with a logical answer to the question: *Why am I feeling this emotion?*. Your mind will tell you that you are feeling this way because of a relationship, your finances, your workload or whatever. Can you relate to this?

Although the story about why you're feeling the emotion may seem logical or true, it is important that you recognize what happens if you go on believing that your life circumstances are the cause of the emotion. The story in your mind usually makes the emotion the result of some external event or set of circumstances, and this assumption usually requires something about your past or future, your body, relationships, finances, career or whatever to need to be 'fixed' or improved before you can let go of the emotion and be at peace. Creating this external change could take hours, days or even years, which is an unnecessary postponement of your peace.

> *In reality, you can let your emotions flow and go much sooner than you may think.*

How Are You Feeling?

Now, for you to be able to answer this simple question, you need to observe whatever emotion is currently occurring within your body. The emotion becomes the object, and you the observer of the emotion, and by observing the emotion you naturally create some space between you and it. From this perspective you can start to recognize, from your first-hand experience, that you are not your emotions. Yes, you have emotions, but the permanent you is not emotional.

You will get very close to freedom from emotional turmoil when you begin to explore your relationship with your emotions. Whichever emotions occur, you can simply let them come and go and experience very little stress or discomfort as they pass through – *if you remember to observe them instead of being them*. The reality is that your real self is untouched by temporary emotions. The permanent aspect of you has never been happy or sad, scared or guilty. Conscious awareness is permanently peaceful and beyond the emotional realm. Let's explore this with a game...

GAME

Watching Emotions

You can play this game whenever you are experiencing an emotion that you would rather not. It is amazingly effective at helping emotions dissolve quickly so you can more easily cultivate your relationship with peace.

STEP #1 **Name It**

Notice what you are feeling right now. Are you feeling happy, sad, angry, anxious or something else? Simply tune in and notice what emotion you are currently feeling.

STEP #2 Locate It

Locate it in your body. Where in your body is it mainly situated? Is it in your stomach, solar plexus, heart or chest or some other place in your body? Locate it now.

STEP #3 Colour It

Once you have located the emotion, give it a colour. Any colour will do. Red, green, violet, black, blue – it really doesn't matter. Just go with your first answer. Colour the emotion now.

STEP #4 Watch It

Now you've named it, located it and given it a colour, simply watch the emotion being there. Imagine you have double-sided eyes: look backward, downward and within to watch the coloured emotion in its location in your body. Just watch it. Remember to keep breathing deeply and in a balanced way as you do this. Continue watching and notice what happens to the emotion. For me, whenever I do this, after a few seconds of watching the emotion always disperses. Like water on a hotplate, or the sun parting clouds, it evaporates and simply disappears!

What Happens When You Observe Emotions?

When you start observing your emotions, you immediately create space between them and the permanent aspect of you. This space gives them a chance to flow and go, which is what they naturally want to do. Furthermore, when you watch your emotions you become aware. When you become aware, you start to experience what your own conscious awareness, beyond the emotional realm, is like. This conscious awareness is always pristinely peaceful, irrespective of what temporary emotions happen to be occurring in your body. More aware of your real self than your temporary emotions, you begin to experience the peace that is always present. Amazing, isn't it? Just doing this simple exercise can help you to be less fearful of your feelings, stop being governed by your emotions and instead enjoy emotional freedom.

Play with the Watching Emotions game for the next week at least. Whenever you notice yourself feeling emotions, whether positive or negative, stop for a few moments to go through the steps of the game: name it, locate it, colour it and watch it. Notice what happens. Remember, there's a big difference between thinking about watching and actually watching. If the emotions don't appear to change then the chances are you have identified with the emotions instead of watching them. By doing this exercise whenever you remember, you are working on discovering that you are not your emotions. This is a massive step towards improving your relationship with your emotions; and the more you practise this game, the more you will benefit ultimately. So go for it!

An Energizing Twist On Emotions

Befriending your feelings can help you to enjoy greater physical health and life success. In fact, I would suggest that many feelings you experience on a daily basis actually exist to help you. As mentioned earlier, emotions are simply 'energy in *motion*' within you, and it makes sense that the more energy you have, the better equipped you are, energetically speaking, to heal yourself and create new successes in your life.

Rather than trying to get rid of your emotions, it can be very productive to harness their innate power. For instance, if your body needs to heal by engaging in a maintenance and repair project, it will often increase its energy levels to help the healing. In this scenario, your body needs extra energy to fix the physical problem.

However, if you try to resist and suppress the energy, you can end up unintentionally inhibiting the healing process!

Said another way, let's say your current energy level is a 5/10, but to heal something your body needs it to be an 8/10. If you notice a feeling and then push it down, you may be inadvertently making it harder for your body to heal. If on the other hand you simply let the energy be present within you, you may well heal more quickly. Personally I have found that since I've been more willing to let emotions occur, the quicker my recovery time has been.

The same goes for if you want to create a positive change in your life in other ways.

Everything you want to create in your life is made up of energy. To meet the universe halfway, the body will naturally raise its energy levels to match the external success that you want. For instance, if your current income requires 3/10 energy levels but you want to make more money, you may find that the thoughts you have about making the extra money you want have emotions associated with them. All too often, the mind will mislabel the emotion – for example, as fear – and you might end up resisting the very energy that you need to create what you want. Again, to let your emotions help you, it is very useful to resist them less and, instead, channel them towards creating the results you want. This will not only lead to freedom from feeling bad, but will also enable you to use your emotions as a powerful manifestation tool.

Play with this…

GAME

Power Breathing
A simple and effective way to harness the power of your emotions is through your breathing. It is common to unconsciously hold your breath whenever you don't want to feel certain emotions. In

doing so, your diaphragm becomes tense and it becomes harder for energy to circulate.

Instead, breathe in deeply through your nose so that your stomach expands and then exhale through your mouth whilst making a gentle 'ha' sound with your breath. You will find that your vitality increases as the energy is freed.

This can be an incredibly energizing and uplifting experience; and also, by raising your energy to meet the energy of the external life problem or opportunity, you will find that you can proceed with courage and conviction.

LET'S SUMMARIZE

Rest In The Power Of Your Real Self

Ultimately, you are only ever upset because you have lost touch with your real self – your still silent conscious awareness. By this I mean that you've become lost in thinking and stopped being aware of the presence of your consciousness. By allowing your emotions to be present within you, by watching them and breathing to let them flow, you will find that feelings your mind has labelled as negative can actually be very empowering and give you the inner strength required to go for and attain your goal.

Feelings that your mind may have previously thought were fear could become your friend.

Enjoy the benefits that come from befriending your feelings. By doing this, life circumstances lose their power to negatively impact you. Not because you deny or ignore reality, but because you become connected with your conscious awareness, which is beyond the surface-level appearance of reality.

Resting within the peace that resides within you, your life becomes liberated. You enjoy a sense of serenity, irrespective of how you happen to be feeling. From this more present and peaceful state, your body finds it easer to heal and you are free to pursue your desires with passion. It's a genuine win-win.

*"Three things
cannot be long hidden:
the Sun,
the Moon,
and
the Truth."*

BUDDHA

CHAPTER FOUR

Shining a Light on the Story

• • • •

WHY YOUR PAST OR FUTURE NEED NOT IMPACT YOUR PEACE

ONE OF THE MAIN REASONS WHY PEOPLE THINK SO MUCH IS THAT THEY BELIEVE THE STORY IN THEIR MIND IS REAL. Well, it isn't! Your stories about your past, your current circumstances and future only exist in your mind, not in reality. And once you fully *get* this, you can more confidently release your grasp on the need to think all the time, start to take your mind less seriously and laugh your way to freedom.

My Overactive Imagination

When I was a child I snuck into the television room late one evening and watched the movie *Jaws*. It scared me to death! For weeks afterwards I couldn't sleep; I was convinced that the big shark from the movie was hiding in my bedroom wardrobe, waiting for me to go to sleep before it came out to eat me! Now, looking back on it I can't help but laugh at the thought of a giant fish living in my wardrobe, but it felt so real at the time; I genuinely couldn't sleep for the angst and apprehension.

When my parents told me the shark in my wardrobe wasn't real, it was just my imagination, I didn't believe them because it *felt* so real. But they spoke the truth and gave me one of the most important lessons of my life. I now know that my problems exist mainly in my mind, in either my imagined past or future, but rarely, if ever, in the real world of this moment.

> *What if much of the emotional stress negatively impacting on your health and peace of mind is very similar to the shark in the wardrobe? What if, although the problems feel real, they exist more in your imagination than in reality?*

The Light Relief From Seeing The Light

Words cannot describe the relief that came to me the day I discovered that my memories of the past, however bad or sad they may be, were only accessible now via my imagination. The same goes for my fears of the future; for years I'd quite literally been scared by my shadow, my imagination. Knowing that the past and future were both nothing more than imagined stories in my mind made therapy to let go of my problems, and meditation to think less, so much easier.

> *Thankfully, to enjoy more peace you don't need to become a time traveller, able to change the past or future. You just need to learn to be more present.*

Unfortunately, millions of people live their entire lives not recognizing this simple truth. They go through their days going over their past or pre-playing future scenarios in their mind, again and again and again, suffering from unnecessary stress, ill-health and struggle in the process, simply because they are in their heads and thinking about the past and future, missing the peace of the present moment.

Your Body Doesn't Know The Difference

Numerous scientific studies have now discovered that, biochemically speaking, your body cannot tell the difference between what is happening in the real world and what is just in your mind. What this means is that, even if you are only thinking about a stressful situation, your body still experiences the same negative physical reactions as it would if these events were actually happening in reality.

Quite remarkable, I'm sure you'll agree! The implications of these findings are hugely significant when it comes to self-healing and serenity. Not only does it explain why so many people on the planet are experiencing physical problems, it also validates the importance of learning how to think less and be more present.

Bitter Pill?

Now I appreciate this might be a bit hard to swallow at first, especially if your problems feel real and appear to be happening now. But for the sake of your health and happiness, I invite you to notice that much of the stress and unease you experience is caused by thinking too much about the past and future.

• • •

Meet Mandy, who had been emotionally taunted by past events for over twenty years…

> I came to Sandy's retreat having been troubled by negative emotions relating to three people for over twenty-two years. These memories had impacted my weight and I'd suffered from anger and depression. After working with Sandy I felt unburdened and completely relieved of the pain I'd been carrying.

Mandy discovered during our meetings that the things she considered to be problems were not problems in reality, but stories in her mind. She let go of over twenty years of pain when she realized that she was causing herself unnecessary stress by continuing to think about what had happened in her past. I showed her how to be here now, and she explored the difference between being present and being in her head thinking about the past. She saw that she was not a victim to a past she couldn't change, and with practice, this gave her the choice to stay in the peace of the present moment rather than stepping back into the pain of her past stories.

No Problems In My Room

My spiritual teacher once shared a story that helped me to let go of my past more easily.

There was once a psychologist based in New York who was retiring after a highly successful career. During an interview about his career, a journalist asked him to share the biggest life lesson he'd learnt from working with thousands of clients over the decades. His reply was certainly not what the journalist expected.

What the wise psychologist said was that there had never been a single person who had ever had a problem in his therapy room. He went on to explain that his room was always safe and secure. There was a comfortable chair to sit on and pretty plants around to provide a lovely setting. But despite everything being perfectly well in his therapy room, every person he saw in there would 'leave the room' – that is, leave the present-moment experience of being in the room – by going into their mind and imagination to remember and recount problems, none of which were actually happening in the therapy room in the here and now. Incredible, isn't it!

Waking Up From The Maya Nightmare

In ancient teachings, the 'story' that I've been discussing is often referred to as the 'maya', which in Sanskrit means 'illusion' or 'dream'. To be honest though, for some the maya is more of a nightmare! It is especially so if a person unwittingly puts all of their attention on the endless supply of problems that the mind can invent.

Now, I appreciate that thoughts and feelings can make the maya appear and feel very real, but they don't mean that it *is* real. Most of the problems that you think about on a daily basis, as we've seen, exist in your mind but not in the reality of this present moment. The more present you become, the less you engage in thoughts about life and the more you experience the fullness of life itself. You come to see that the story in your mind is always about the past and the future, and that by putting your attention on your temporary, time-based thoughts and emotions, you neglect the beauty and perfection of the present moment.

Ill-health may continue, money might be short this month and someone somewhere might have decided they don't like you. Nevertheless, these things only become a problem when you become less present by engaging in judgemental thinking about them.

Freedom from problems can be a reality for you – if you learn to think less about the stories in your mind.

Perhaps contradictorily, in the next chapter we are going to spend time exploring being present in much greater detail. As a sneak preview though, I invite you to start to notice that *this* moment, right now, is happening. You are reading this page and everything about this moment is actually OK. It might even be better than just OK! You may be clothed and fed, sitting comfortably and enjoying the experience of reading *this* word. Become super-attentive to this moment and you may begin to notice that there is a quiet peace present within you.

Being present is not only about noticing what's happening now. As you are going to discover, it's also about becoming aware of your presence, your being, your inner quietness and your stillness. Because as you put your attention on *this* moment, you will find that to start thinking about any problems you have to take attention away from it. Thinking is often an unconscious action, and many people are firmly in the habit of putting their attention on thoughts about the past and future. But if you play with being super-attentive to now, you will notice the dance that happens between this moment and the stories happening in your mind.

Denying Reality

One of the most common objections to letting go of the story is that it can feel as if you're denying reality. Thinking about your problems can make them feel very real and to ignore them can feel like burying your head in the sand.

However, this objection depends on your definition of reality. I would suggest that reality is, literally, what's real: and what's real is what's happening right now. Everything beyond the immediate experience of right now is made up by your mind. To access the past or future you have to engage your imagination. By this rationale, to start thinking about the past and future is to deny what's real right now. So the only way that you can ultimately deny reality is to engage in thinking about things that are not happening now.

By 'not thinking', I do not mean that you should become passive and stop taking proactive steps to improve situations that are causing you concern. What I mean by 'not thinking' is that you don't think too much about the things you perceive as problems. Negative thinking only invests energy in what you don't want and makes you more prone to continue recreating these things. By reducing the amount of thinking you're doing you can actually free up this energy and significantly improve your body and your life. Not only that, but you will also get to wake up and live in truth, as opposed to existing in your only relatively true mind-made version of reality.

GAME

Story vs Reality

In your journal, write down a problem that you are currently dealing with. This problem could relate to a relationship, your health, your finances or anything else. Then take a few moments to actively think about the problem in your mind.

After about one minute of thinking about the story, answer these questions:

- Where am I right now?
- What colours can I see right now?
- What sounds can I hear right now?
- What am I physically touching right now?
- Is this problem happening right now?
- What is it like if I notice this moment is happening?

Story vs Reality Example

THE STORY: *What is the problem?* I'm going through a relationship break-up. The person I'm in love with has decided they don't want to be with me and I am feeling sad and alone without them in my life.

THE REALITY: *Where am I right now?* I am currently sitting on a chair in my garden. *What colours can I see right now?* I can see green trees moving in the breeze and blue sky overhead with some clouds floating by. *What sounds can I hear right now?* I can hear birds singing. I can hear the buzz of traffic in the distance. There is also silence happening. *What am I physically touching right now?* My bottom is pressing against the chair that I'm sitting on. I'm holding my pen and I can feel the journal that my hand is resting upon. *Is the problem happening right now?* No, my ex-partner is not here with me now and the argument was only continuing to happen in my mind. *What is it like to notice this moment is happening?* This moment is bright, clear, fresh, still, full of potential and peaceful.

> *You can see that you have a choice: you can put your attention on the mind-made dream, or on living reality.*

Using this exercise can help you to see that whenever you are thinking about a problem, you are missing the present moment. Your attention is not on all of the colours, sounds or physical sensations, but instead is on the negative story in your mind. The implications of this can be enormous!

As you play with this exercise, you will probably notice that your mind attempts to convince you that you need to start thinking about the problem so that you can figure out a solution. However, if you continue to be brave by being present, you might find that letting go of problem-based thinking often allows things to improve, in a very effortless and expansive way. You will be more gentle, loving and kind in your actions and your new way of being will be reflected in your external life circumstances.

Move Beyond Problems For Good

Just because I'm saying that life can be problem-free, I don't mean that it won't challenge you. On the contrary, in my experience life continues to includes challenges; but as I've let go of my personal story, my relationship with life has improved massively. It is challenging, but I know that ultimately nothing is wrong and everything that happens helps me to wake up from the illusion and enjoy more peace, love and freedom.

Life moves from being problem-full to peace-filled.

By being present you can free yourself from harmful stress as you resist life less. You stop holding onto the past and fighting what might happen in the future. The mind is the master and the body is the servant; or, put another way, the body follows the mind – and the natural by-product of a peaceful mind is a resting body. A resting body is able to heal as it naturally wants to, which enables it to be in balance, function as it was designed to, age well and experience true vitality.

By letting go of the judgemental thoughts happening within your mind, you can even experience life as though there is nothing wrong. Life is perfect. You are perfect. Life is complete. You are complete. Life isn't broken, and neither are you. You rest in the knowing that better health, peace of mind and happiness are your birthright, your most natural way of being. This will come to you when you stop resisting life and, instead, focus your attention on enjoying the peace that occurs naturally when you are fully embracing the present moment you're in.

I believe that we are not on this planet to focus all of our attention on fixing, changing and improving, but that we are here to learn how to love fully. By learning to accept life by cultivating an 'inner yes', you can use everything that happens to help you to learn how to enjoy more peace, love and freedom. The choice can be yours.

"Be content with what you have now;
rejoice in the way things are now.
When you realize there is nothing lacking,
the whole world belongs to you."

LAO TZU

CHAPTER FIVE

Thinking Makes
You Miss Life

. . . .

THERE ARE NO PRESENT-MOMENT THOUGHTS

THINKING TOO MUCH PREVENTS YOU FROM ENJOYING THE PEACE THAT IS ALREADY PRESENT WITHIN YOU. Life is happening right now. Now is all there is. It is forever new and fresh and full and vibrant. Everything that exists within reality exists only now. Now is the only moment that exists. The only moment *you* exist. And the only moment in which you can *ever* experience inner peace.

This chapter is about letting go of the notion that anything needs to change, be fixed or improved before you can enjoy peace. It's about no longer thinking that your peace is dependent on your past or future, by learning to let this moment be enough.

Thinking Something Is Wrong

Growing up I went to nursery, primary school, secondary school and then university. I gathered a huge number of concepts about life and was constantly encouraged to become a better thinker. I was taught that if I had a problem, a solution could be found by thinking it through. Yet, despite becoming really good at thinking, my life continued to consist of problems and peace eluded me.

Nobody ever told me that the underlying cause of my problems was the very act of thinking itself. So after university I went on to spend thousands of pounds on personal-development courses to change my mind and enjoy the problem-free peaceful existence that my heart yearned for. But the more I tried to change and improve myself, the more I found things that needed fixing and improving!

After countless attempts to find peace through the next personal-development course, a friend made a passing comment that changed my perspective completely. She said that she was 'a victim of personal development'. This really resonated with me. I saw that all of the courses I had attended had a hidden assumption at the heart of them that implied something was wrong with me and that I had to fix, change and improve my mind in order to make my life better.

Hidden in the depths of most people's minds is the belief that 'something is wrong with me and my life'. I've observed that this belief operates silently, out of sight, and leads to feelings of fear, discontentment and angst. Speaking personally, it caused me to resist my life and never feel fully contented with how things were, or how I was. And most relevantly to the context of this book, I've discovered that this is the hidden belief that causes the compulsion to think.

The mind loves a problem and becomes very active in its attempts to find a solution. So as long as you go on believing that there is something wrong, then you will feel compelled to think too much. But the good news is that it doesn't need to be this way.

Imagine I could reach inside your mind and remove the belief that something is wrong. What is that like for you? How would you feel if you knew nothing was ultimately wrong? Whenever I ask audiences to do this at my talks, the usual response is that they feel 'free', 'calm' or 'content', and I see lots of smiling faces as they notice their minds becoming quieter.

Much of this book from now on aims to help you to become present and reconnect with your peaceful presence. My intention for helping you to do this is that you rediscover the fullness and perfection of the present moment. You will find that when you are present you naturally transcend the hidden belief that something is wrong and instead experience the nirvana of now. Sound good? Let's begin by exploring the difference between thinking and being here now.

The Hidden Barrier To Experiencing Life

Life is always present. It truly is. However, you can end up missing it if you are in your head thinking. This is because although life exists now, your mind only exists by thinking about the past and future. Thinking acts as an invisible barrier that stands between you and the present moment, between you and the experience of peace. I say "invisible" because most people aren't aware of the impact thinking has on their peace.

Thinking makes you numb to fully experiencing life because your mind is always one step removed from any given experience. The mind cannot experience the present moment; it can only think *about* the present moment. Similarly, the mind cannot experience peace, it can only think *about* peace. So as long as you continue to be in your mind thinking, your peace will remain out of reach.

Are You Postponing Living Fully?

Due to the mind's inability to experience peace, it has no alternative but to postpone it. It assumes that something must be wrong with life now and works tirelessly to find all the things that need to be fixed, changed or improved. It tells you that you must do x, y or z in order to be peaceful and that you need to change your body, your finances, your relationships, your career, your environment … pretty much everything! All before you can enjoy some peace.

Not being aware of this tendency of the mind can cause you to end up victim to its never-ending postponement of your peace. The future never comes. So you can end up waiting for peace your entire life due to your mind's ability to endlessly think up new items to add to your 'things-I-need-to-do-so-I-can-eventually-enjoy-some-peace' list!

Don't get me wrong; I'm not suggesting your mind is against you. Quite the opposite! It believes by helping you to change your body and your life that one day you will be able to enjoy peace. But here lies the problem.

> *Your mind will always put your peace in the future because it cannot experience it now.*

There Are No Present-moment Thoughts

Before I learnt that there was an alternative way of being, I spent most of my days lost in my mind thinking about the past and future. I would think about what had happened hours, days, weeks and even years ago, or mentally rehearse all the things that were going to happen hours, days, weeks or years in the future. Sound familiar?

One of the biggest insights I've gained from countless hours of meditation and guidance from enlightened teachers is this: There are no present-moment thoughts. Let me explain what I mean.

For the mind to talk about something it needs to have happened already. So if you are thinking about the past or the future, you are missing the present moment.

Being present and being peaceful are one and the same. You cannot experience one without the other. Knowing this makes experiencing peace supremely simple and brilliantly clear-cut:

> *You are either in the moment experiencing peace or you're in your head thinking about peace.*

Peace Is Not Present In The Past Or Future

Despite your peace only ever existing now, the potential exists for your attention to slip into the past and future via your mind. Going into the past is only possible if you go into your imagination. The past is nothing more than a collection of old thoughts. Reality, on the other hand, is what's real, right now. (I think this is why it's called *real*ity!)

So if you want to experience real peace, I recommend you don't waste a second intentionally thinking about past moments. You will not find peace there. Nor will you find peace in the future. The future might offer hope, but this present moment delivers you home to the peace, love and joy that is your birthright to experience, explore and enjoy. Remember, even if you are successful in your quest to make your past and future perfect, you can still only ever experience peace *now*. So again, why waste your time deliberately thinking about the past or future if experiencing peace now is what you ultimately want?

This book is all about you *experiencing* peace, and it is impossible for you to directly experience anything truly fulfilling in any time other than now. But don't take my word for it. Take some time to consider your top three best moments of your entire life so far. They will probably have one thing in common – you were present. Time had ceased to exist. You were not thinking about the past or future. Instead, you were giving your full attention to whatever was happening.

The great news is that by learning to be present, much of your life can be as fulfilling as your best moments.

The Glorious Gifts From Being Present

Believe it or not, what's happened in your past or what might happen in your future does not have to impact upon your current levels of peace. When you are fully present there is no time to dwell on the past, complain about the present or wish for more in the future.

You discover that it is much more appealing to be here, in this moment, than to think about the past or future. You notice that thinking about the past and future feels dead compared to the vibrancy of now. You notice that once something has happened, it is immediately in the past. Gone. For ever, even if it happened only a moment ago. You stop holding on to the past or fighting what might happen in the future. You know that nothing in the past is worth thinking about and nothing in the future could possibly bring you more peace than being present.

> *It becomes the natural choice to make the most*
> *of this moment.*

No longer relying on your future to give you anything, you let this moment be enough and, as a direct consequence, experience perfect peace, limitless love and heaps of happiness. Fully present, you are not judging this moment or comparing it to a past or future moment. You experience life as being perfect, whole and complete. You rest fully in the peace that's always present.

TOP TIP Being Present Practicalities

One of the most common confusions about being present is the belief that it means you can no longer talk about the past and future. However, the good news is that you can talk about whatever you want! From an ongoing awareness of the present moment, you are able to talk about what's happened in the past or plan for the future (I do it all the time within the context of my work, when sharing stories about the past and planning my courses and retreats.) However, the main difference is that you remain fully aware of the present moment, and talk about whatever you want from this perspective. The difference is that you don't leave the present moment to re-experience the past as you talk about it. Get the difference? The same goes for future plans – you can be right here, right now, and yet still plan for events in the future.

Exactly how to do this is explained further in the next chapter. By playing with present-moment awareness as you talk about the past or future you will notice that there is a huge difference when it comes to the levels of peace you enjoy. You will be able to talk about past events (even traumatic ones) without any emotional turmoil whatsoever because most of your attention is here, rather than there. You may also find that worrying about the future falls away, as you no longer need it to fulfil you. It is a very freeing way to be.

Now Let's Review The Past Chapter!

If you aren't enjoying as much peace, love, beauty, mystery, fun or happiness as you would like, then it doesn't mean these things aren't already present in your life; it just means you aren't present enough to experience them. By getting out of your thoughts and getting into the present moment, you can experience life as a wonderful gift.

Being present and being peaceful are intrinsically linked. You cannot experience one without the other. Enjoying peace by living in the present moment is supremely simple and clear-cut: You are either in the moment experiencing peace or you are in your head thinking about peace. The choice can be yours.

GAME

Peace Postponers

Explore what you believe needs to happen so you can experience peace of mind. Be honest with yourself when answering the following questions. Avoid editing your thoughts between your head and your hand. It is important that you see your unedited thoughts, so you can challenge the ones that might be postponing your peace.

1. **What do I think needs to change about myself so I can experience peace?**
   (Things to consider include the shape, weight and health of your body, your intellect, your skills, your achievements, your failures, your past and your future)

2. **What do I think needs to change about my life so I can experience peace?**
   (Things to consider include your health, your relationships, your finances, your security, your responsibilities, your time pressures, your career and your living environment)

3. **What do I think needs to change about myself in order for me to be 100 per cent loveable?**
   (Things to consider include the shape, weight and health of your body, your intellect, your skills, your achievements, your failures, your past and your potential)

4. **What do I think needs to change about my life in order for me to love it completely?**
   (Things to consider include your health, your relationships, your finances, your security, your responsibilities, your time pressures, your career and your living environment)

Bonus Question

5. **What ideas do I have about enlightenment?**
   (Things to consider include: What is an enlightened person like? How do they behave? What happens in their mind? Do they have thoughts? Do they have emotions? Is enlightenment possible in this lifetime for me?)

Having answered the above questions, now consider: *Are any of your answers conditions that are postponing your peace?* By this I mean: are you waiting for things to be different, fixed or improved before you can enjoy peace, love and contentment? If you have found conditions, then great! It is important that you become aware of the things you believe must happen because these are the very thoughts that you need to be willing to let go of in order to enjoy more peace now.

The truth is that nothing needs to change about you or your life for you to experience peace. It is just a conditioned belief that tells you otherwise. Your mind will always put your peace in the future because it cannot experience it now. Yes, it can think about peace, but because it cannot experience it, it will constantly tell you things need to be different for you to experience peace.

You can end up missing peace your entire life if you believe your misinformed mind.

Freedom from problems and peace for life requires you to be OK irrespective of what's happening in your body, your mind and your life. In the next chapter I will share the missing piece of the peace-of-mind puzzle. You will learn one of my favourite ways to play with being present. In doing so, you will be able to reconnect with the peace that's always present.

*"Become conscious of
being consciousness."*

TIMOTHY FREKE

CHAPTER SIX

The Missing Peace of the Puzzle

• • • •

EVERYTHING EXISTS WITHIN A CONTEXT OF PEACE

FREEDOM FROM THINKING TOO MUCH BECOMES POSSIBLE IF YOU UNDERSTAND AND APPLY WHAT I'M GOING TO SHARE NOW. For me, it was the missing piece of my peace-of-mind puzzle; so much so that after I properly got what you are about to get now, enjoying real peace in the real world became a living reality for me. There's no reason why the same cannot be the case for you too.

Being present is more than just noticing what you can see, hear, feel, smell and taste now. What you put your attention on matters hugely and is often overlooked. Peace can continue to elude you if your attention continues to be scattered. As people learn to be present in their daily lives it is common for their attention to jump from one thing to the next as they attempt to be aware of whatever is currently happening; this is very often a reason why people miss the peace that's always present. To avoid this, you can learn how to be attentive to the underlying, subjective reality of the present moment.

On The Surface Of A Chaotic Ocean

Like the surface of the ocean, your thoughts, emotions, body, career, relationships, money and all other aspects of your external world are constantly changing. That's what they do. Thoughts happen, emotions flow, the body does its thing. New people enter your life as others leave. Careers change, political parties rise and fall and economic climates can change as quickly as the weather. Due to all these aspects of your body, your mind and your life being in a constant state of flux, and to a large extent, out of your direct control, it is no wonder you don't find much peace there.

The Power Of Your Personal Attention

The good news is that there is one thing in life that you have a high degree of control over: namely where you put your attention. This is something that nobody else can control. It is something that your external life circumstances need not dictate. Irrespective of what's happening to your body or in your life, you have the power to choose what you put your attention on in any given moment. This being the case, the next obvious question to ask is: *Where can you put your attention so you experience the most peace now?* The answer to this question is nothing less than enlightening!

> *Ultimately, there are only two things you can focus your attention on: namely, the outward content or the inward context of your life.*

Let's assume for a moment that the entire universe exists within the room you are currently in. In that room there might be furniture, flowers, light fittings, your telephone and other belongings. The term I use to refer to all these things is STUFF. Now, for all the stuff to exist, there has to be the context of SPACE. In fact, there has to be more space than stuff, otherwise the stuff wouldn't fit in the space. And although the stuff can come and go, the space that it inhabits is constant and unchanging.

CONTENT	CONTEXT
Stuff	Space

As you read these words you may become aware of SOUNDS around you. There might be the sounds of a clock ticking, birds singing, the hum of traffic in the distance, the shimmering of leaves outside your window, music playing or people talking nearby. For these sounds to exist, indeed for you to hear anything, they have to happen within a context of silence. Sound needs silence. Even if you are surrounded by noise, there is SILENCE so you can hear the noise, and that silence resides within your awareness – now and always.

CONTENT	CONTEXT
Stuff	Space
Sounds	Silence

Furthermore, the content of your current experience also includes MOVEMENT: the movement of your chest as you breathe, the movement of your fingers as you progress through this book, the movement of the trees outside your window as the breeze continues to blow. Yet, again, the content of that movement happens within a context of absolute STILLNESS, a stillness that is untouched by any movement, ever.

CONTENT	CONTEXT
Stuff	Space
Sounds	Silence
Movement	Stillness

So we've discovered that the content of your life, including all of the stuff, sounds and movement, all happens within a context of still silent space. Not only that, but the content comes and goes and is changing whereas the context is constantly present and unchanging. Incidentally, the same is true within your mind; the movements of your thoughts and emotions all occur within a constant context of still silent space.

Now the million-dollar question:

> *Where do you tend to focus most of your attention through-out your day – on the content or the context of your life?*

Almost everyone, when I ask this question, sees clearly that they put most of their attention, most of the time, on the content of their mind and lives.

Naturally You Feel What You Focus On

So if you put all of your attention on that which is moving and changing, you will most likely experience a sense of instability and unease. However, reconnecting with the peace that's always present requires you to learn to put your attention on that which never moves or changes and is permanently still and silent.

Making this shift in where you put your attention immediately reconnects you with your birthright. Peace, contentment, love, happiness and so much more – it's waiting patiently for you. Waiting for you to become aware of its already present existence.

> *Your real self is the still silent conscious awareness that is aware of this moment happening. And that awareness is already at peace, perfectly contented and full of love. You are not separate from that, but by thinking about the past and future you can take your attention away from it.*

Remember This From Now On

Looking for peace in your mind (by having no thoughts), in your emotions (by only feeling positive), in your physical body (by it being healthy and looking how you think it should), or in your career, money, relationships and any other aspects of your external life circumstances DOES NOT WORK. You don't need to take my word for it; your own life experiences can be evidence enough! So if you have not found peace by looking to change, improve and perfect your body, your mind or your life, then it's probably time for a new strategy.

You feel what you focus on. By focusing on things that constantly change and are out of your control, it is not surprising you haven't been feeling peaceful. However, by putting your attention on stillness, on space and on silence you naturally experience peace.

It really can be as simple as that.

LET'S PLAY A GAME

Noticing The Moment

Let's play a game to help you experience what I've been talking about. There are three golden rules for this game that you must adhere to if you want to reap the immediate benefits:

- **RULE #1: You can't play this game wrong**.
  So just play like a child. I remember as a kid I used to play for hours with a cardboard box and a couple of spoons, imagining that I was in a boat. I couldn't do it 'wrong' because I was just playing. So don't try to get this right, just play and explore innocently and see what happens.

- **RULE #2: You can't do it later.**
  By this, I mean you can only do it now. So don't try to analyze what I'm asking you to do or plan to do it later. Instead, just do it, immediately.

- **RULE #3: You can't think about doing it.**
  You can only do it. If it isn't working for you, then you are in your mind thinking about it, instead of being in the moment experiencing what I'm inviting you to notice.

Happy with the rules? Great, let's get started!

As you are reading this I am going to assume you have a page in front of you, either printed or on a computer screen. I want you to keep looking at the page as you notice your left shoulder. To notice it you don't need to look at it or move it, just tune in and notice your left shoulder.

OK? Easy? Perfect. Let's continue.

Now notice your right foot. Again, you can keep looking ahead at the page as you notice your right foot. You can keep reading. You don't need to wiggle your toes or anything like that. You can simply take your attention to your right foot and notice it now.

OK? Still easy? Great. Let's continue.

Now, without trying to figure out what I'm asking you to do, I want you to notice the space between you and this page. Just do that now. You don't have to look around between you and the page, just keep looking ahead and simply notice that the space exists. It's been there the entire time; all you are doing now is noticing that it is there as you continue to keep your gaze on the page.

Still easy? OK, let's continue playing.

Now I want you to notice the space around the page. Don't look directly around the page; keep looking directly ahead as you notice this space. Notice the space around the page for a few moments before continuing.

You are doing great.

Now I want you to notice the space in the entire room. Like a switch in your awareness, let your attention notice the space in the entire room. As you do that, I want you to notice what it's like to do this.

What's your inner experience like as you notice the space in the entire room? Remember, keep your gaze forward and don't look around the room trying to find or see the space. Trust me, it's there. All I want you to do is notice the space in the room. As you continue to do this, what word or words could you use to describe what your experience is like as you notice the space now? I've asked literally hundreds of people to do this. Common answers include: 'calm', 'peaceful', 'still', 'open', 'expansive', 'light', 'comforting', 'home' and 'freeing'. As you notice the space in the entire room, what word(s) could *you* use to describe what it's like to notice the space?

TOP TIP **Trust Your First Answer**

Don't stop noticing the space to try to describe it; that will start you thinking and stop you experiencing. Just notice and trust your first words.

Let's continue. Now I want you to notice that *this moment is happening*. That you are sitting where you are, reading *this* word. Observing *this word* being read. And now *this word*. Simply notice that this moment is happening. What's it like to quietly notice? To do nothing other than gently watch this moment occurring. What words could you use to describe what your experience is like as you do this? Common words used to describe this are 'calm', 'peaceful', 'quiet', 'still', 'spacious', 'open' and 'free'.

Experiencing What It's Like To Be Aware

Well done. This exercise helps you to become aware by noticing. When you become aware you become present, because your awareness that is noticing is always present. Your awareness can only ever be aware of *this* moment. Even if you are not aware of your awareness, due to getting distracted by thought and emotions about the past and future, your awareness remains permanently aware of this moment – only and always – a silent watcher watching from behind your eyes. Furthermore, when you become present, you immediately start to directly experience what your awareness is like. Because awareness is by its very nature still and silent and spacious, you start to experience exactly that. Or in other words, you start to experience more calmness, peace, quietness, expansiveness and more.

For Any Doubts

The mind is movement. It consists of thoughts about the past and future that come and go. Your mind cannot mimic the experience of still silent space. This means you are genuinely beyond your mind, in the present moment, when you are placing most of your attention on the presence of still silent space now.

Knowing this helps to avoid confusion as to whether or not you are present, allowing you to be confident that if you are ever thinking about whether you are present in that moment, you can be sure that you're not!

TOP TIP **Practice Makes Permanent**

Play with this game as much as possible. Notice the space between you and other people when you are talking to them, or the space between you and your computer. Notice the space around objects, whether that's people, your cup of tea or your TV. Notice the space in the entire room you are in, whether that be the office, the supermarket or your kitchen. Notice, notice, notice! Remember the three golden rules and pretend that it's your first time every time you do it.

You may notice that each time you do it there's more peace than there was a moment before, when you weren't aware. Perhaps more importantly, you will notice that it works every time. Why is this so important? Because you have the opportunity of discovering that when you become aware, you become present, and when you are present, you experience peace. How amazing is that?

Peace Never Left You; You Left Peace!

Playing with this game consistently will help you to notice that you experience a presence of peace every time you become aware of the underlying reality of the present moment. That your awareness is the permanent aspect to you and your awareness is still, silent and peaceful. Beautifully, you can discover that peace never left you; rather, you left peace, simply by taking your attention away from this moment by engaging in thoughts and thinking.

Permanent Peace Starts Now

Desiring permanent peace is natural and wonderful. The remarkable news is that permanent peace *is* possible. Yet, despite this exciting possibility, always remember …

> *Life is only ever happening now, so peace for life is 100 per cent about being peaceful now.*

If you want your experience of peace to be permanent then simply make it your number one priority to be inwardly attentive to still silent space now.

Let the future take care of itself. The only thing that matters is where your attention is right now. Are you putting most of your attention on movement or stillness, sound or silence, stuff or space? If you find yourself caring whether your peace is permanent or not, it means that your attention has slipped away from the presence of peace now and gone into the future via your mind. Be here now. Be still now, and you will find that your peace is permanent – as it always has been!

"What you are looking for
is what is looking."

ST. FRANCIS OF ASSISI

CHAPTER SEVEN

From Failure To Success in Seconds

• • • •

HOW CULTIVATING CONTEXT AWARENESS CAN CREATE AN INNER STATE OF SUCCESS

"THE KINGDOM OF HEAVEN IS WITHIN" IS A COMMON MESSAGE SHARED BY MANY SPIRITUAL TEACHERS. If given the choice, I believe anyone would choose heaven over hell any day. However, the big question is *how?*

My own explorations into finding nirvana within this lifetime have included meditating day and night for ten weeks on the island of Patmos, followed by a further fourteen weeks in the mountains of Mexico, and more meditation retreats since then. During these extended periods of meditation and of course during my daily meditation routine, I've discovered that the content–context model shared in the previous chapter can offer a roadmap for finding freedom from problems and enjoying what can best be described as heaven on earth. So let's continue the exploration by diving further into the context of … everything!

In the previous chapter we discovered that content – stuff, sound and movement – exists within a context of still, silence space. And by putting your attention on the context you can think less by discovering the peace that is always present. But the benefit of exploring the context of your mind doesn't end there. In fact, it is only the beginning!

CONTENT	CONTEXT
Stuff	Space
Sounds	Silence
Movement	Stillness

Let's continue by considering this: On which side would you say the mind actually exists – the content or context side? When I ask audiences this question, it is common for people to assume that the mind is the context; however, this is not so. To encourage a fresh perspective, I often go on to ask: How do you know you have a mind? After a pause, the answer I usually get is something like: 'Because I'm aware of it'. So by that rationale, the mind is the content, whereas the context of the mind is your conscious awareness.

Your mind may not feel the content, but that doesn't stop it being the content.

Without awareness there would be nothing to be aware of the mind. Or, said differently, you would have no way of knowing what your thoughts were if it was not for the conscious awareness that was aware of them. Obvious thing to say, perhaps, but it is fundamental when learning how to think less.

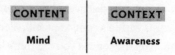

CONTENT	CONTEXT
Mind	Awareness

Most people are fixated on the content of the thinking mind because they have forgotten that thoughts exist within the context of awareness. They have become so focused on the content of their mind that they leave little, if any, attention to notice the awareness that is aware of their mind. They are focused on the birds so much that they miss the sky. In doing so, they become so lost in thoughts that they end up missing the divine presence of still silent peace that all of their thoughts exist within.

> *Have you ever noticed that you still exist even when you are not having any thoughts?*

One of the fun findings that can be found when playing with the counting-thoughts exercise in Chapter 2 is that thoughts come and go. Not only that but, more importantly, if you are super-alert, there is space between your thoughts. What is that still silent space? What continues to exist even when no thoughts are happening? The answer: awareness. Your conscious awareness is the permanent aspect of you that is the permanently open doorway to the eternal gifts that exist within the present moment.

When Does Now Exist?

Moving on from the mind, let's take a moment to consider a question relating to time, namely: *Where does time actually exist?* To answer this I invite you to consider how you access the past and future. Think back to when you were reading the previous chapter. Where does that moment exist now? It is in your mind, right? How about the moment in time when you will eventually finish reading this book? To go to that future moment, you can only go via your mind, using your imagination. This must mean that time exists in the mind. Yes, I agree there is clearly the transition of days and nights, of physical aging and of days and months on calendars. However, any time other than right now can only be accessed via the mind and imagination.

This can be a very exciting discovery if something bad has happened in your past or if you've been worried about the future. It means that if it is not happening right now, then to feel bad about it you've had to go into the past or future by thinking about it in your mind. And by learning to stay aware of *this* moment you can let go of the past and future and enjoy the serenity of *this* second.

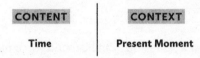

CONTENT	CONTEXT
Time	Present Moment

Furthermore, this means that if you want to learn how to be more present, you can do so by cultivating the habit of being aware of the still silent spacious context of this moment, a practice that I like to call context awareness.

The Judgement Game

When the mind and time get together they can have a dramatic effect on your serenity and success. The mind can end up using the past and future to compare and contrast how it was and how things could be better in the future. When it does so, it engages in what I refer to as the Judgement Game.

Drawing on time, the mind loves to make sense of life by putting what happens into a box. By judging life events as either good or bad, better or worse, and right or wrong, it uses this judgement to decide whether you should allow or resist whatever has happened, is happening or might happen. This isn't an obvious problem if you end up on the good, better and right side of the equation, but it can lead to stress, negative emotions and a life full of problems if you end up on the bad, worse or wrong side of things.

> *"There is nothing either good or bad,*
> *but thinking makes it so."*
> **WILLIAM SHAKESPEARE**

Judging life negatively leads to an 'inner no' towards life rather than an 'inner yes'. The inner no creates a conflict between your inner and outer life experience that is detrimental to your peace and prosperity. It creates an inner sense of angst and inhibits creativity by making you more prone to living and operating using the fight–flight survival areas of your brain. Life in this situation becomes very black and white, and much energy and effort is often used to force life to look how you think it should.

Unfortunately, the negative knock-on effects of the Judgement Game don't end there. Saying no to life events also often causes you to feel compelled to resist what's happened, is happening or might happen. This resistance to life not only puts unhealthy stress upon your body, but is also the hidden cause of many negative emotions, such as frustration and fear.

CONTENT	CONTEXT
Judgement	Is'ness
Problems	Perfection
Inner No	Inner Yes
Resistance	Allowing
–ve Emotions	+ve Emotions

The Positive Side-effect Of Is'ness

Now for some very good news! Something very magical happens when you are courageous enough to withdraw your attention from judgemental thinking. Life stops being good or bad, right or wrong or better or worse, and you get to see that everything just is. Yes, on the surface things may appear to be bad, wrong or worse, at times, but you cannot deny that there is simultaneously what can be described as a mysterious is'ness to life.

Still silent spacious awareness does not break, or become sick or bad. It is always perfect, whole and complete exactly as it is. It is beyond judgement because it is beyond the mind. Said another way, the context is the no-mind.

In my experience, the more I put my attention on the context, the more I experience an inner perfection to life, irrespective of whether or not my mind judges life as being perfect. In fact, for the record, my mind continues to this day to judge many aspects of my life as not being perfect. Despite the opinions of my judgemental mind, by choosing to actively place my attention within on still silent space using context awareness, I find that I do what it takes to deal with whatever may arise in my life while simultaneously experiencing the inner perfection and beauty of the presence that resides with conscious awareness.

You don't ignore what's happening in your life. You ignore the judgements your mind has about your life. As a result, you do what it takes to improve your body, life and world while simultaneously being aware of the inner presence of peace and perfection.

Believe it or not, you can enjoy a massive amount of serenity and success by recognizing the is'ness of life. By putting your attention on the context you rest within an inner yes that allows this moment to be exactly as it is. The result: peace and a whole host of other positive emotional experiences as well, including contentment, joy and love.

From Failure To Success In Seconds

How do you know when you are successful? Is your success dependent on your bank balance? The size of house you live in? The number of cars you own or being recognized by receiving awards? What is success for you?

Although this book can help you to enjoy more external life success by accessing more confidence and creativity and getting more done with less stress, this part of the content–context model is more about feeling successful on the inside. Which, for many, is a major factor in feeling successful.

Having worked with many highly successful business people at my clinics and retreats, I have observed that true success is not an external thing. Many of the millionaires that I've worked with have accomplished more in life and business than most people would dream of. Yet, despite the external success, they don't necessarily feel successful yet.

CONTENT	CONTEXT
Failure	Success

One of the main reasons for this highly confusing predicament is that, despite their riches, they don't *feel* successful on the inside because their focus is entirely on the limited content of their life. No external possession or position in society can fulfil you if you are missing a huge aspect of your real self and reality. It costs nothing to rest within the fullness of the context of life. By shifting your attention using context awareness, you can immediately engage with a sense of abundance, completeness and success that is free for everyone, doesn't require you to prove your worth and has nothing to do with your qualifications, skills or opportunities.

Inner Stillness = Outer Success

Being still doesn't mean you become idle: quite the opposite in fact! When you are inwardly aware of stillness, your mind quietens and you naturally become more present, intuitive and creative. You enter a highly effective state of being that many sports people or artists know very well and call 'the zone' or 'flow', in which you are fully present and your thinking mind is out of the way.

From the here and now and with a clear mind you will be amazed at what can be accomplished. Personally, I rest in this still silent state pretty much all of the time – when writing my books, working with clients at my Mind Detox clinics, running residential retreats and teaching my Academy Practitioner courses – because life is so much more effective and enjoyable when I do so. In fact, at the time of writing this book I've been simultaneously writing three other books, without stress or struggle and while running events and maintaining a social life!

Success becomes easier when you are still. By still I don't mean physically standing still. I'm referring to being attentive to the presence of still silent space within your awareness. Doing so makes you present, and from the perspective of the here and now there is no unhelpful stress, even when you're faced with a big workload.

When fully present, you give your full attention to whatever it is you are doing right now; and because the now is immediate, there is always very little you can do right now. For example, writing a book is a daunting and potentially stressful task, but writing this *word* is very easy and takes very little effort. By remaining present as you progress through whatever work requires your attention, you deal with what's in front of you, now, and then move on to the next thing and then the next … and before you know it, you've written a book, built a business or achieved something pretty spectacular, all with very little stress and while enjoying a great deal of serenity. You get to properly enjoy the journey and experience the destination as a bonus, not a necessity. With context awareness life becomes free-flowing and easy.

The Opposite Of Control Is Freedom

Until a person develops the skill of context awareness, they can end up suffering from what can be best described as *one hell of a life!* They will spend their days missing life because they will be too distracted by incessant thinking about the past and future. Their enjoyment of life will go up and down depending on which side of the Judgement Game they happen to end up on. If they end up on the bad, worse or wrong side, then life can end up feeling like a never-ending series of problems that need to be fixed or avoided. They will never quite get 'there'.

When things don't go to plan they will often end up resisting life, which as you've discovered leads to unnecessary stress and heartache. Not to mention a sense of being a failure, irrespective of what they achieve, as their mind convinces them that they are never quite 'there' yet. In order to make things better and get 'there', people lost in the content side of life often end up overly controlling, manipulating and managing life in a bid to make things better, which all contributes to prolonging the unfortunate cycle.

Thankfully, on the other side, freedom is waiting for anyone willing to search out a new way of relating to life. The more you can learn to let life be, by resting in the peace that resides within the context, the less you need to control what happens. It becomes clear that the opposite of control is freedom. By that I mean that the less you need to control life, the freer you are. And the freer you are the more serene and successful you naturally and automatically feel.

If given the choice I don't know anyone who would choose hell over heaven. If you take a step back and look at the two lists that we've created, I hope it is much clearer that being lost in the content is very unappealing when compared to resting in the context of your awareness. When you come back to the context you become present and experience the perfection of is'ness and the serenity that comes from disengaging judgmental thinking and instead saying an inner yes to life.

Summary Of The Content–Context Model:

CONTENT	CONTEXT
Stuff	Space
Sounds	Silence
Movement	Stillness
Mind	Awareness
Time	Present Moment
Judgement	Is'ness
Problem	Perfection
Inner No	Inner Yes
Resistance	Acceptance

CONTENT	CONTEXT
Stress	Serenity
-ve Emotions	+ve Emotions
Failure	Success
Control	Freedom

The Link Between Problems And Thinking

There is a direct relationship between judging life as bad, wrong or worse and the compulsion to overly think. The mind loves a problem. It becomes highly active on finding a solution. So if you continue to judge life circumstances as wrong, then your mind will continue to work overtime. However, if you let life be as it is, you will immediately find that there is less of a need to think, that your mind becomes quiet and that serenity and success are your reward.

Cultivating Context Awareness

Moving your attention from the content to the context is one of the most important skills you can ever develop. It can free you from problem-based thinking for good, and give you the living experience of heaven on earth.

So how can you make the change? One of the most powerful ways to cultivate the habit of context awareness is, of course, meditation. However, despite meditation being widely known as a powerful antidote to thinking too much, there are many myths about it that can make people feel more frustrated than free. So to ensure that you don't suffer from the same misunderstandings, let's explore these myths in the next chapter...

*"The moment you put your mind aside,
you have entered into
the world of meditation.
When you are in deep meditation,
you feel a great serenity."*

OSHO [2]

CHAPTER EIGHT

Ten Myths About Meditation

• • • •

WHY MEDITATION IS EASIER THAN YOU THINK

CLOSED-EYE MEDITATION SERVES MANY PURPOSES, FROM STRESS RELIEF TO SPIRITUAL AWAKENING. Personally, I started meditating because I was fed up with my mind working overtime. I wanted peace and through meditating regularly I have become less focused on the movement of my mind and much more aware of the inner peace that is always present.

Reconnect With Your Real Self

Meditation helps you to become aware of the essence of what you are. It works by helping you to change your relationship with your mind. You stop being your mind – being fully engaged in thoughts and emotions – by learning to watch without engagement. Through the practice of watching, you start to become aware of the awareness that is watching. You notice that your awareness is still, silent and untouched by any temporary movement of the mind – completely out of the way of any external threat. With regular practice and guidance, you can live free from fear; fully aware you are one with the source of love.

TEN MYTHS ABOUT MEDITATION

Despite meditation being so simple, and having such big rewards, there are some myths about it that can stop people getting started or make them quit before they get to reap the benefits of regular meditation. In this chapter I want to talk about what these myths are and teach you a simple way of meditating to help you get started.

MYTH #1 Meditation is Difficult

Practised correctly, meditation could be the easiest and most enjoyable thing you ever do. For something to be difficult, it has to involve effort, struggle, stress and stamina, and the truth is that meditation requires the exact opposite. There is no effort because you are learning how to do nothing. There is no struggle because you are not forcing anything. There is no stress because you are not resisting anything and there is no need for stamina because the main purpose of meditation is to rest!

MYTH #2 I Must Still My Mind

'I can't meditate because I can't stop my thoughts' is one of the most common reasons I hear from people who've tried meditation but quit. However, what's important to understand is that thoughts are a natural (and necessary) part of meditation.

When you meditate your body gets rest. When the body rests it heals. Healing is an active process – stress is released and healing is being undertaken. Due to the mind–body connection, activity in your body is reflected by activity in your mind – which takes the form of thoughts. Having thoughts when meditating is therefore a sign that healing is taking place in your body. Healing your nervous system is a fantastic by-product of meditation. It is not useful, therefore, to resist having thoughts when meditating. To resist thoughts is to resist healing! Instead, let the healing process happen, as it naturally wants to, by not resisting the existence of thoughts.

> *Thoughts are a necessary part of meditation. Thoughts are natural. Thoughts are OK!*

With practice, you will learn how to put more attention on still silence rather than the movement of your thoughts. When this happens, you won't care if thoughts are happening or not because your attention won't be on them.

MYTH #3 If Thoughts are OK, then it's OK to Think

Although having thoughts is OK, I am *not* recommending that you *intentionally* think your way through every meditation. There is a big difference between having thoughts and thinking. When you are meditating you want to let thoughts flow through your awareness without engaging in them through the act of thinking.

Thinking occurs when you stop observing your thoughts and start being them. When you are thinking, you are in the thought stream. You are in the dream. Engaged in the story of your mind, you are having an imaginary conversation with your friend, planning what you're going to have for dinner, or whatever.

> *Thinking is very similar to falling asleep.*

When you are thinking, you are essentially lost in your mind. You are no longer present, nor consciously aware of your real self. Thinking is a habit you learn to do less of through the regular practice of meditation. Be gentle on yourself if you find yourself thinking when meditating. It's just a habit! When you become aware that you've been thinking, simply come back to being alert, present and watching.

MYTH #4   I Have to FEEL Peaceful

Be careful not to fall into the common trap of thinking a peaceful meditation is better than an emotional one. Similar to thoughts (in Myth #2), having emotions when meditating is a sign of stress releasing from your body and healing taking place. Also, remember that emotions are only ever temporary, but the presence of peace is permanent. Emotions exist within the *content* of your mind, but your peace is the *context* of your mind. It is a fascinating experience when you begin to notice that you can simultaneously have a 'negative' emotion whilst being perfectly at peace. Regular practice of meditation will reveal and develop this freeing experience.

MYTH #5   Meditation Stops when I Open my Eyes

Most of your day will be spent with your eyes open, so thankfully the little flaps of skin that you call your eyelids do not need to impact upon your peace. Peace is experienced when you put your attention on the still silent space within your awareness. You can direct your attention with your eyes open or closed. One goal of meditation is to develop the habit of effortlessly having some of your attention looking inwards to still silent space at all times. Eyes open or closed – it need not matter.

MYTH #6   It's Pointless Trying because I Fall Asleep

Your body will do what it needs to do when you meditate – if it needs sleep then you will sleep. That is perfectly fine and if you continue to meditate regularly you may find that the need for sleep reduces as you learn to be less stressed during daily life. If you find yourself falling asleep every time, though, then you might want to experiment with the following ways of staying more alert during meditation:

- Meditate at times of the day when you know you are more likely to be alert
- Sit more upright (you can still be comfortable, if you use the right support)
- Do some exercise before meditating so that you are physiologically more awake.

MYTH #7 I Have to Breathe a Certain Way

Many forms of meditation encourage participants to focus on their breath. There are also many that don't. Focusing on the breath can help you be less focused on the mind, but it is certainly not an absolute necessity when meditating. The form of meditation I use myself does not rely on the breath, but I do find breathing, generally speaking, to be very useful indeed!

MYTH #8 I Have to Concentrate Hard

Peace, joy, love, contentment and freedom are all natural by-products of being consciously aware, as opposed to being unaware, lost in your mind thinking. The good news is that meditation takes very little effort, because it takes zero effort to be aware. You are already aware. Awareness is what you are – whether or not you are aware of it yet!

MYTH #9 Visualization is the Same as Meditation

Meditation helps you to experience more peace by moving your attention away from the movement of your mind to the still silent space residing within your awareness. Guided visualizations, on the other hand, require you to focus your attention on the mind. So although guided visualizations may by fun, they do not lead to permanent peace.

Remember, the mind is movement so it cannot mimic stillness or silence. So when your attention is on still silence you are resting beyond the mind. Being beyond the mind means you are beyond limitation, beyond judgments and beyond problems. Being beyond your mind means you are resting in the heart of all that is good.

MYTH #10   It Takes a Long Time to Enjoy Any Benefits

You start benefiting from meditation from the moment you begin. You might not experience immediate peace or joy, but your body will get a chance to rest, release stored stress and heal. This myth reminds me of a story. A 70-year-old man wanted to learn to play piano. His son questioned what the point was because it takes so long to learn. However, the piano-playing pensioner wasn't persuaded to quit. Instead, he simply told his son that if he started now he'd be a much better piano player by age seventy-five than if he didn't start at all!

I love this story because it is very much the same for meditation. It may take a little time to experience highly noticeable changes, but if you start, and keep doing it regularly, you can be sure you will be experiencing much more peace, love and happiness over the coming months and years, compared to if you never start at all.

BONUS MYTH   Meditation is Boring

Whether something is boring or not is a matter of opinion, and your opinions exist in your mind. By ignoring thoughts and emotions associated with boredom you can more quickly enjoy mind mastery.

"Most people are asleep.
They're born asleep, they live asleep,
they marry in their sleep,
they breed children in their sleep,
and they die in their sleep –
all without ever waking up.
They never understand the loveliness and
the beauty of this thing
that we call human existence."

ANTHONY DE MELLO [3]

CHAPTER NINE

Closing Your Eyes to Wake Up

• • • •

HOW TO KEEP CALM AND CARRY ON

GET MOTIVATED TO MEDITATE! Mind mastery is the ability to stop thinking whenever you want. You use your mind as the amazing tool that it is, and then 'put it down' when you're done. You are attentive to the context of stillness and think only occasionally, when it is useful. Being a master of your mind is not about manipulating it. Rather, it's about having the ability to direct your attention towards or away from the mind at will.

As a result, a master of the mind knows that thoughts are nothing to fear and that no thought has any power to negatively impact their mood or lovability. They enjoy freedom from problems because they no longer take their mind so seriously. It is a wonderfully calm way to live – although it does take courage.

Heros Wanted, Apply Within

The path of waking up from unconscious thinking by returning to stillness has been known by many names over countless years, with my personal favourite being the Path of the Hero. The more I meditate the more I can appreciate why it's been called this.

Thinking all of the time is a habit, a destructive one at that. In my opinion, thinking is one of the most harmful habits on the planet. It causes a huge amount of conflict, self-violence, stress and suffering.

> *Have you noticed how people experiencing inner peace don't hurt others? Peaceful people know we are all connected by the same one consciousness. So to hurt another person is to hurt oneself.*

Yet, despite all the pain, fear and conflict linked with innocently forgetting Who You Are (e.g. peace-filled consciousness), thinking you are your thoughts, and buying into the endless judgements of the mind, it is a familiar habit, and with familiar comes a sense of (false) security. For many, stopping to think can seem like a scary prospect. So we cling to thoughts and thinking, as we might to the side of a swimming pool before we've learnt how to swim. Let me take a moment to reassure you.

Let go of thinking as you would at the side of the pool and I promise that you will discover that you float. In what, you might ask? The safe serene context of the mind, which I've been directing you towards over the past few chapters. As you let go of the mind you naturally rest back into the deep, clear and infinitely loving sea of consciousness that has been holding you your entire life. For many, it feels like coming home.

Using Meditation For Context Awareness

Meditation provides a safe arena to practice letting go of thinking too much. You can sit in the safety of your own home and in the comfort of your favourite chair (but not so comfortably that you will inevitably fall asleep!) and explore what it is like to rest in the still silent context of your conscious awareness. Cultivating the habit of context awareness requires the investment of your time and the courage to stop and meditate for about 10 minutes, 2 times each day. Irrespective of how busy your mind says that you are and how much you need to get done, you do it anyway. With this kind of commitment, you can move mountains.

What Is CALM?

Conscious Awareness Life Meditation (or CALM for short) is easy to understand and enjoyable to use. You can learn it in a few minutes and get practising immediately. CALM can help you to change your relationship with your mind by becoming more aware of the context of life. The natural by-product of you thinking less and being aware of your awareness is a happier, more peaceful and loving life.

> CALM *combines the power of 'Om' with nine pure intentions and focus points.*

For years now, scientists have known that everything in the physical world is vibrating. Ancient teachings have known this vibration to be the 'Om'. 'Om' is the vibration of creation. It is the first movement from stillness, the first sound from silence and the first something that comes from nothing. Whatever you marry 'Om' up with in your mind you can help to bring into creation. With CALM you align 'Om' with nine pure intentions such as 'peace', 'clarity' and 'wisdom' that you bring to your mind (see page 111 for full list).

To complete each CALM thought there is a location within or around your body upon which to focus your attention when you think the words. These focus points make the CALM thoughts more powerful because they act as energy magnifiers for the pure intentions.

It has been said that 'you are what you seek.' These pure intentions are like seeds within you, however, they have become hidden under the content of thoughts and thinking. Using CALM regu-

THE CALM DIAGRAM

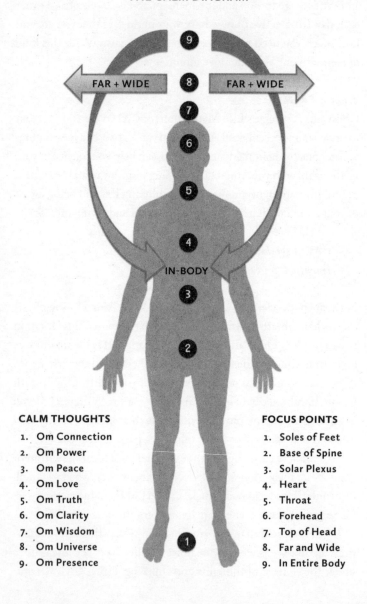

CALM THOUGHTS

1. Om Connection
2. Om Power
3. Om Peace
4. Om Love
5. Om Truth
6. Om Clarity
7. Om Wisdom
8. Om Universe
9. Om Presence

FOCUS POINTS

1. Soles of Feet
2. Base of Spine
3. Solar Plexus
4. Heart
5. Throat
6. Forehead
7. Top of Head
8. Far and Wide
9. In Entire Body

larly is like watering these positive seeds of life and giving them light to grow. Over time you can bring the nine positive intentions into your everyday experience.

The Nine CALM Thoughts With Focus Points

1. OM CONNECTION (Focus Point: Soles of Feet)
2. OM POWER (Focus Point: Base of Spine)
3. OM PEACE (Focus Point: Solar Plexus)
4. OM LOVE (Focus Point: Heart)
5. OM TRUTH (Focus Point: Throat)
6. OM CLARITY (Focus Point: Centre of Forehead)
7. OM WISDOM (Focus Point: Top of Head)
8. OM UNIVERSE (Focus Point: Far and Wide)
9. OM PRESENCE (Focus Point: In Entire Body)

How To Meditate Using CALM

Sit comfortably, close your eyes, be gently alert to now and notice whatever thoughts are happening in your mind for approximately one minute.

1. Then think 'OM CONNECTION' with your attention on the Soles Of Your Feet ... let go of the words and focus point, and gently be alert to now until you notice that you've been thinking other thoughts.
2. Then think 'OM POWER' with your attention at the Base Of Your Spine ... let go of the words and focus point, and gently be alert to now until you notice that you've been thinking other thoughts.
3. Then think 'OM PEACE' with your attention In Your Solar Plexus ... let go of the words and focus point, and

gently be alert to now until you notice that you've been thinking other thoughts.

4. Then think 'OM LOVE' with your attention In Your Heart … let go of the words and focus point, and gently be alert to now until you notice that you've been thinking other thoughts.

5. Then think 'OM TRUTH' with your attention In Your Throat … let go of the words and focus point, and gently be alert to now until you notice that you've been thinking other thoughts.

6. Then think 'OM CLARITY' with your attention in the Centre Of Your Forehead … let go of the words and focus point, and gently be alert to now until you notice that you've been thinking other thoughts.

7. Then think 'OM WISDOM' with your awareness at the Top Of Your Head … let go of the words and focus point, and gently be alert to now until you notice that you've been thinking other thoughts.

8. Then think 'OM UNIVERSE' with your attention Far and Wide … let go of the words and focus point, and gently be alert to now until you notice that you've been thinking other thoughts.

9. Then think 'OM PRESENCE' with your attention In Your Entire Body … let go of the words and focus point, and gently be alert to now until you notice that you've been thinking other thoughts.

Either repeat the cycle (1-9) or if you are ready to finish your sitting meditation session slowly open your eyes.

Repeat each CALM thought for a period of approximately one minute before moving onto the next. Or for longer meditation sittings you can repeat the same CALM thought for up to five minutes or more. Remember to leave some time between each CALM thought – the golden rule is to only focus upon your CALM thought when you notice that you've been thinking about something else. This way they will help you to be present and notice the context awareness. Using each CALM thought for one minute each will add up to a 10-minute closed-eye CALM sitting.

THE 4-WEEK CALM CHALLENGE

Thinking too much, getting stressed and missing the present moment during the rush of modern life is a habit. But thankfully, so is worrying less, sleeping better and being more peaceful and happy.

CALM helps you to make the transition from having all of your focus and attention on the content of your life (your ever-changing thoughts, emotions, body and life circumstances) ... and instead rediscover the present moment peace-filled context of life. For the best start in making conscious awareness your new habit, do the 4-week CALM challenge:

10 Minutes Of CALM, 2 Times Per Day, For 4 Weeks

Good times of the day are before breakfast, midafternoon, before dinner and before bed. Little and often is the best way to get the best results from CALM – which is great news because everyone has ten minutes spare here and there throughout their day. So if you are ready for a new way of thinking, feeling, living and loving, start your 4-week challenge today! (Also, visit my website to gain access to online resources to support your practice of CALM.)

TOP TIP **Enjoy Moments Of CALM**

You can also use your CALM thoughts with your eyes open. Choose one of the CALM thoughts and think it whenever you remember throughout your day. Just think it and let it go and move on with your day until the next time you remember. By doing open-eyed CALM you can bring more serenity and conscious presence into your everyday life.

Let Go, Let Be, Let Love
Frustration occurs during meditation if your mind decides that it wants whatever experience is happening at this moment to be different. Or in other words, if you engage with the thoughts, emotions or physical sensations that naturally want to happen as you sit and let your body rest, by saying an inner no. Remember, your body will heal whenever it is given the chance. These experiences are very often stress releasing from your nervous system as your body repairs and rejuvenates itself. To resist what happens when meditating is to resist healing!

It is much wiser to let go and let be. One way to do this is to intend to let the moment be enough, exactly as it is. What's it like to play with that now? Let this moment be enough. Take a break from trying to fix, change or improve anything and let whatever is happening just be. For me this is very calming; it's a relief to let go of any engagement with trying, straining or controlling. To let this moment be enough is to enter a state of unconditional allowing. Such a shift in intentions is what is required if you want to be more gentle and loving towards yourself, other people and your life.

Noticing Still Silent Space
As you meditate, you may become aware of a quietness or stillness or openness. This is your conscious awareness, your real self. It is good to let your attention move to the stillest quietest part of your experience so you can cultivate a more intimate relationship with your real self.

As I mentioned earlier, ideally I recommend 10–20 minutes of meditation two or three times every day: in the morning before breakfast, before your evening meal and before bed. Through short and regular stints of meditation throughout your day you can learn to be more present, release stored stress and become increasingly aware of a constant context of still silent peace. It's worth it!

BONUS TIP#1 **Meditation Works!**
That's why it's been around for thousands of years. And it will work for you if you keep doing it. The only reason you will stop meditating, and miss out on all the benefits, is if you believe your mind when it says one of the following thoughts:

> *I don't have enough time today*
> *I'm having too many thoughts*
> *I'm not feeling peaceful*
> *This isn't working*
> *I think I will stop and try again later*

Don't Be Fooled
If you ever have any thoughts like the ones above that could talk you out of meditating, then I recommend you laugh at them and continue meditating. Freedom comes from not being ruled by your conditioned mind. Happy meditating!

BONUS TIP#2 **Take Inspiration From Others**
Thinking about quitting your meditation practice? Then take inspiration from others who have made the commitment to meditate regularly and experience the boundless benefits. Turn to page 147 to read a number of inspirational stories from people just like you who have transformed their lives using meditation.

"To the mind that is still,
the whole Universe surrenders."

LAO TZU

CHAPTER TEN

Techniques for Thinking Less

• • • •

THINK LESS BY BECOMING A CONSCIOUSNESS EXPLORER

BEING THUNK IS A HABIT OF A LIFETIME. Like all habits it can take time to break free from your old ways by consistently cultivating your new, more desirable behaviours. I recommend that you waste no time overly thinking, and instead set the intention to master context awareness so that you can enjoy all the benefits outlined in this book so far.

To help you to do this, Chapter 10 includes ten highly effective techniques for thinking less, being present and noticing the still silent spacious presence that exists within your awareness, always now.

Today you embark on a new role in life – being a consciousness explorer!

TECHNIQUES IN YOUR
THINKING LESS TOOLKIT

TECHNIQUE #1 3C Vision
Focus in and spread out your field of vision

TECHNIQUE #2 Soul Windows
Take time to look into the eyes of another

TECHNIQUE #3 Noticing Nirvana
Play with the possibility that nothing is wrong

TECHNIQUE #4 Inward Gazing
Direct your attention inwards towards your heart

TECHNIQUE #5 Balanced Breathing
Focus on the breath as it flows in and out

TECHNIQUE #6 Sensory Awakening
Take your attention to your senses for serenity

TECHNIQUE #7 Resonance Revolution
Rest aware of the still presence of life

TECHNIQUE #8 Silence Speaks
Be aware of the silence that allows sound

TECHNIQUE #9 Enlightened Eye
Look at life from the centre of your skull

TECHNIQUE #10 Air Aware
Look at life from the one-eye

One-Pointed Practice

Some of these techniques will resonate with you and you will find that they work almost immediately. Others may not make any sense, or you may find them more difficult. My advice: read through all ten techniques and apply them as you go. Find the ones that work for you and be one-pointed in practising them over the next six weeks. During that time you will make some amazing discoveries and, more importantly, you will make massive shifts in your habit of thinking versus your new and improved habit of context awareness.

TOP TIP **Just Do It!**

Remember there is a difference between thinking about and doing in the moment. For these techniques to work, you have to simply do them. If you overly analyze them you will be thinking too much again, and will end up missing the experience that these techniques can guide you into. Take inspiration from the very wise Master Yoda from *Star Wars*:

> *"Do or not do. There is no try."*

TECHNIQUE #1 **3C Vision**
Focus in and spread out your field of vision

USING YOUR EYES FOR A CHANGE: 3C vision is a remarkable way to clear your mind and feel calm, confident and content in any situation. By using your eyes in a certain way, you can activate the parasympathetic nervous system, which quietens the mind and can help you to begin to notice still silence. In fact, I would go as far as to suggest that it is very hard to think while engaging 3C vision! But don't take my word for it – try it now.

Instructions:
1. Pick a spot on a wall to look at, ideally above eye level at about a 45 degree angle, so that as you look at it, it feels as though your vision is bumping up against your eyebrows.
2. As you stare at the spot on the wall, effortlessly let your mind go loose and focus all of your attention on the spot. At this point you may find yourself wanting to take a deep breath in and out. Let yourself do so.
3. Notice that within a matter of a few moments, your vision will begin to spread out. You will begin to see more in the peripheral than in the central part of your vision.
4. Now, pay more attention to the peripheral part of your vision than to the central part of your vision. Notice colours, shadows, shapes and so on. Notice what you see on the left and right, above and below. Keep using your peripheral vision – don't look directly at anything.
5. Continue for as long as you want while noticing how it feels. Notice if your mind has become more still.

With a little practice you will be able to use 3C vision as you go about your day – when reading, out walking, chatting with people, pretty much any time you want to stop thinking and feel calm, confident and content.

TECHNIQUE #2 Soul Windows
Take time to look into the eyes of another

The eyes are often called the windows of the soul, and looking into someone else's eyes can be profound. It encourages you to recognize that, although you have different physical bodies, there is an essence to both of you that is the same and is not even separate. You can recognize and rest within an inner essence that is beyond the physical body, beyond time and beyond separation. I have felt a lasting connection with the people I've done this exercise with.

Instructions:
- To do this easy yet profound exercise, either sit or stand directly in front of a partner who is willing to do it too. For a prolonged period of time – ideally ten to twenty minutes – simply look into your partner's eyes. Yes, that's right. Look into the other person's eyes without speaking and while doing your best not to make any distracting facial expressions. Just look.
- As you do, consider this: What is watching? What within them is being watched? What are you looking at? What are you seeing? Can you become aware of the still silent awareness within you that is watching? Is that separate, or one with their consciousness?

This is *not* a staring competition and you are allowed to blink whenever you need to, so remember to stay relaxed throughout.

TECHNIQUE #3 Noticing Nirvana
Play with the possibility that nothing is wrong

The belief that there is something wrong is a major hidden source of angst. It is the subtle belief that makes people resist what happens and, in the process cause themselves an awful amount of unnecessary stress. You cannot control everything that happens, but you can heal the belief that makes what happens so stressful. If you ever find that you are in need of a serene moment, use this technique to bring you back into touch with the inner peace that's present.

Instructions:

- Imagine that I could reach inside your mind and pull out the belief that something is wrong. That's right, like magic, the belief that there is something wrong with your body, your life or your world could be completely removed from your mind.
- What's left? Seriously, try that experience on for a few moments and notice what it is like.

The results from the many people I've played this game with have been remarkable. In their eyes I see immediate relief, and comments include that it feels 'free', 'a relief', 'peaceful' and 'expansive', to name only a few. What is it like for you to take a moment to pretend that nothing is wrong? By looking at life through a lens in which nothing is wrong, you can start to notice the nirvana that is there, all day every day.

TECHNIQUE #4 **Inward Gazing**

Direct your attention inwards towards your heart

What is it like if you pretend you have double-sided eyes and look outwards whilst simultaneously gazing inwards towards your heart?

Instructions:

- To do inward gazing, find something outside and in front of you that you can use as an external point of focus. This might be a door handle, the corner of a picture frame or a spot on the wall.
- Then, while maintaining some attention outwards on that external point of reference, pretend that you have double-sided eyes and look back, in and down towards your heart area.

- As you do this, notice what happens to the thoughts in your mind. Do they quieten? Do you become aware of how still it is within you now?

Inward gazing is a fantastic way of cultivating a more consistent inward attentiveness. You will find that you can take your attention inwards, and place it upon your heart, and still interact very effectively with the external world. In fact, many people who practise this technique find that they become more present than when all of their attention is outwards on stuff, sound and movement.

Play with inward gazing when you are speaking with friends, working at your computer and walking in nature. It can help you to become aware of the presence of peace within, as well as honing your skills at context awareness.

TECHNIQUE #5 Balanced Breathing
Focus on the breath as it flows in and out

Balanced breathing has been found to cause both heart and brain coherence. An incoherent mind is one that is thinking all the time – the 100,000 thoughts per day I mentioned earlier.

On the other hand, a coherent mind is one where the two hemispheres are in harmony with one another and the mind is naturally more still.

Instructions:

- Balancing your breathing couldn't be simpler. As the name suggests, just easily and comfortably breathe in for the same amount of time that you breathe out. For example, breathe in for a count of five and then breathe out for a count of five.

- Continue for five minutes or as long as you feel comfortable. If at any point you feel light-headed, stop and return to your normal breathing pattern and take your attention to your feet to help feel grounded.

TOP TIP **Breathe Properly!**

Most people don't breathe properly, which prevents the natural release of tension and places the body under unnecessary stress as it tries to operate with less oxygen than it would like.

Try this quick test: place the palm of your hand on your stomach now and breathe in deeply, noticing what happens to your belly when you breathe in. Does it go in when you breathe in or does it expand outwards when you breathe in? For most people the stomach goes in when they breathe in, when in fact, breathing properly requires the exact opposite! For your lungs to expand fully, the diaphragm needs to drop, which causes the stomach to expand outwards.

You may find it useful to set aside a particular time in your day to do your balanced breathing. Alternatively, you can just do it whenever you notice yourself lost in the content of your mind. Good times of the day include while having a shower in the morning, when in transit on buses or trains, or while meditating.

TECHNIQUE #6 **Sensory Awakening**
Take your attention to your senses for serenity

The more you are in the moment the less you are in your mind. Furthermore, the more you become actively aware of what is happening now, the more you experience the still silent fragrance of what your awareness is like. Sensory awakening involves taking your attention to your senses to fully see, feel, hear, smell and taste whatever is occurring right now.

Instructions:

- NOTICE WHAT YOU CAN SEE. Only look, without labelling. Look at the colours. Look at the shapes, at the textures. Notice the light. Look at the distance between objects. Be aware of the space. Focus on individual objects, noticing things about them that you may previously have missed. Now expand your vision out into the periphery of what you can see. See all that is to the left of you and to the right of you. Now see all that is above and below your eye level.

- NOTICE WHAT YOU FEEL. Now notice all that you are touching. Notice your clothes, the ground and the chair, if you are sitting on one. Feel the air dancing all around you, all so lovingly touching every part of you. Feel the temperature. Feel how it feels to just breathe. Feel life inside and around you. Just feel.

- NOW LISTEN TO THE SOUNDS. Tune in. Avoid labelling or judging. Just listen. Gently listen to the silence that allows the sounds, and the silence that allows the silence. Be super-stereo, tuning into sounds that you may previously have been missing. Are there birds or traffic in the distance? Is there a ticking clock? Or can you hear the sound of the air travelling up and down your nostrils? Tune in and listen as if the volume had been turned all the way up.

- NOW NOTICE THE SMELLS. Take your attention to your nose by feeling the air as it enters your nostrils. Simply being fully aware of the air moving in and out of your nose can be an extremely enjoyable experience if you are fully attentive and involved in each breath. While you are at it, focus fully on what you can smell right now. Is the smell sharp or dull, high or low, sweet or sour? Take your attention to your nose and notice how, when you do so, your mind becomes clearer.

- NOW NOTICE THE TASTES. Void of food, what tastes are already present within your mouth? Also play with sensory awakening with different foods and drinks. When you do, totally tune into your taste buds, the textures of the food and, of course, the tastes. What is it like to temporarily hold the liquid in your mouth before you swallow? How does the food feel between your teeth as you chew? The simplest foods and drinks can be the most delicious experience if you eat consciously.

By filling your attention with your senses you leave less attention for the thinking mind. Naturally you think less and become more fulfilled with whatever you are seeing, hearing, feeling, smelling and tasting.

TECHNIQUE #7 Resonance Revolution
Rest aware of the still presence of life

Now it is time for a more advanced and subtle technique. Still silence resides within every thing in physical existence. Every tree and every animal, and even everyday objects like the glass you drink from and the house you live in, have a resonance of stillness to them.

To become present and attentive enough to notice the silent resonance of life is to begin to see with fresh eyes the underlying nature of reality. And as you do so, it is impossible not to discover the underlying nature of your real self.

Instructions:
- Take time and attention to look at inanimate objects with the intention of tuning in and noticing the still silence that resides within them.

- Decide what object you wish to consciously explore and look at it. As you do, intend to notice the inherent stillness it has to it. It is still and sitting within stillness. Even if it is moving, there is still an exquisite stillness to it, if you are open to seeing.
- Look without labelling and just be with the object fully. Feel its presence and, as you do, notice your own. This technique can bring your world to life and help you to fall back in love with the beauty all around.

TECHNIQUE #8 Silence Speaks
Be aware of the silence that allows sound

Before I discovered context awareness I had always thought that there was only either 'noisy' or 'quiet', but in reality, for there to be any sound there has to simultaneously be silence. Sound odd? It did when I was first told this, but it's true if you can be attentive enough to *hear* the silence. Inner silence is something so familiar that it is easy to forget that it's present all the time. Children know it well, adults less so, due to being so distracted by the content of sounds.

Take a moment to consider this: if there was the context of noise, would you be able to hear anything? Or do you need silence for sound to exist? Even if you were at a rock concert and the music was so loud that you knew your ears were going to ting the following day, for you to hear the sound of the music there must be the constant existence of silence. Otherwise the context would be noise and you wouldn't be able to hear anything! The truth is that there is a constant underlying presence of silence that allows you to hear sounds, and that silence resides within you.

Instructions:

- One of the easiest places to locate the silence is within your ears. Take your attention to any sound you can hear right now and gently begin to notice that there is an inner silence that enables you to hear it.

- Focus less on what you can hear. Instead, turn your attention to the one within you that is listening. Gently be aware of the listener within to find the presence of now.

Another way of noticing silence is to locate your attention at the centre of your skull, then slowly move your attention outwards towards your ears. For some people, there is a moment when they notice the silence; it becomes clear and blatantly obvious. Playing with putting your attention on the silence within you is a highly effective way of withdrawing your attention from your thinking mind and placing it instead on the context. As you feel what you focus on, focusing on silence helps you to feel more serene.

TECHNIQUE #9 Enlightened Eye
Look at life from the centre of your skull

The enlightened eye exercise is an absolutely fantastic way to practise becoming more aware of the awareness that remains aware throughout your day. Instead of having all of your attention outwards on stuff and movement, you move your attention inwards to look out from the centre of your skull.

The enlightened eye is a gate that leads within, to inner realms of still space and higher consciousness. When doing this technique you cannot help but become more conscious of the silent awareness looking outwards. As you become aware you start to experience your own awareness, which, as we've covered before, is still, silent and spacious.

Instructions:
- The enlightened eye exercise requires you to notice what it is like to look out from the centre of your skull.
- To do this, pretend that your eyes have magically moved backwards and you can look out from further back in your skull. As you do, notice if your mind becomes quieter and you become aware of the silent watcher within.

`TOP TIP` **Watch From Your Heart**

Looking out from the centre of your skull can be difficult. If this is the case for you, play with what it is like to use your heart. In order to do this, pick an object and watch it normally with your eyes while also having the intention to watch it with your heart. Intending to watch from your heart area naturally draws your attention inwards, which can allow you to connect with the presence within. Keep an open mind (and heart!) and see what happens.

`TECHNIQUE #10` **Air Aware**

Look at life from the "one-eye"

Following on from the enlightened eye exercise is my personal favourite technique: air aware. It may seem like an obvious question to ask, but how many eyes would you say you are looking out of? It goes without saying that you see two eyes when you look in a mirror and other people see two eyes when they look at you. But more intriguingly, how many do you see out of from your own point of view?

"I am looking out from one eye", is the response I usually get from the many budding consciousness explorers I've asked. Take a moment to notice this reality. Although you have two eyes, you are looking out from a one-eye. Yes, both of your eyes are working, but from your perspective, you are looking out from a frameless window of awareness. Some spiritual teachers refer to this as the eye of God.

Instructions:

- To be air aware is to pretend that you have nothing above your shoulders except for one big eye.
- Play with what it's like to look out at the world from one eye, floating in still silent space. Doing so helps to quieten the mind and reconnect you with your real self, which is unbounded conscious awareness.

Be The Still Silence

Still silence is not something that you have to work hard to find or try to keep hold of. Rather, it is What You Are. Being the still silence is about noticing the living truth; that you are not separate from the presence of peace, but instead that you are one with presence and that it takes no effort to rest within the beyond-words brilliance of Who You Are.

True serenity and success comes from fully knowing and consciously experiencing Who You Are.

"The world will continuously challenge you. Take peace with you everywhere you go by making being peace your priority."

ECKHART TOLLE [4]

Putting a Price on Your Peace

. . . .

THE ETERNAL "GAME" FOR FREEDOM FROM THINKING TOO MUCH

Summary Of The Key Messages Of THUNK!

- Instead of spending years trying to change your mind so that you have only positive thoughts and emotions, you can experience more serenity and success by moving beyond conventional thinking and changing your relationship with your mind.

- You do not need to postpone your peace until a future moment in time when things are how you think they should be.

- The quality or quantity of the thoughts and emotions passing through your body–mind need not negatively impact your serenity and success.

- It is not your thoughts that trouble you, but the commentator on your thoughts that does.

- Although peace can only be experienced now, your mind always postpones peace because your mind is one step removed from the peace that is always present.

- Experiencing peace now requires you to be beyond the mind by being aware of your real self.

- Your real self is the permanent, still silent spacious conscious awareness that is aware of your temporary thoughts and emotions, physical body and external life circumstances.

- Conscious awareness is beyond the physical, mental and emotional realms, void of problems and already serene.

- By placing your attention on the still silent space within your awareness you move your attention away from the constant chatter of your mind, and instead become present and experience presence.

- Inner serenity is the direct result of letting this moment be enough, exactly as it is.

- External success is more easily attainable when you are plugged into the still silent source of creativity, intuition and inspired action.

- Being peaceful does not mean you become passive. By letting your attention rest inwards on still silence, it is still possible to proactively make positive changes to your life.

- By meditating regularly, ideally three times every day, you can change the habit of uncontrollable thinking to a new habit of context awareness. In doing so, you can experience ever-increasing levels of serenity and success, for life.

Although we have looked at and learnt about these very powerful insights and already started to explore experiencing more serenity and success, this final chapter is by far the most important. I want to prepare you for enjoying long-lasting and ever-increasing levels of peace and prosperity in your life. This is because, although we are coming to the end of this book, your life continues. Unexpected physical conditions may arise, misunderstandings may occur, deadlines may be tight and other challenges might present themselves.

However, irrespective of what life brings, you need to be willing to take your attention away from your overactive thinking mind and, instead, place it on the still silent peaceful presence residing within your conscious awareness. A choice that becomes possible if you…

Make Peace Your Priority

When you know how to experience peace, the main thing that stands between you and your peace is your priorities. Take a moment to consider:

How important is my peace?

What things are more important than my peace of mind? Is experiencing peace now more important than having a different past or a better future? Is peace more important than having better health? Is money more important than peace? What else might I be making more important than my heart's greatest desire of peace?

Put A Price On Your Peace

Although this may sound rather unspiritual at first glance, I'm serious about putting a monetary value on your peace. I used to get awfully upset over a £30 parking ticket. When I did, I was unwittingly valuing my peace of mind at a mere £29.99 or less. I was willing to exchange my precious peace for the price of a parking ticket. How silly! You need to make your peace more important than your perceived problems. Doing so is one of the bravest and universally beneficial things you can ever do.

COMMON REASONS PEOPLE
DEVALUE PEACE

To help you avoid making similar mistakes, I'm going to share some of the most common things that people (unintentionally) make more important than their peace of mind:

REASON #1 Being Right

Stop trying to be right – it's not only stressful, but more often than not it's pointless. The more you become consciously aware of the present moment and rediscover your real self, the more it becomes clear that there is a big difference between relative and absolute truth. That there is only one absolute truth, which is beyond all belief systems and only able to be experienced first-hand. Everything else, beyond the direct experience of truth now, can only ever be a relatively true belief existing in the conditioned mind.

Truth Is Always True

Remember, beliefs are only sometimes correct, in some circumstances, for a select few, in limited locations, at certain times. Absolute truth, on the other hand, is always true, in all circumstances, for everyone, in all time and space. Any belief you have may appear correct to you, but I can guarantee that someone else on the planet believes the exact opposite. This is why people can argue over beliefs, but never over the experience of truth. There is only one truth. Truth has no opposite. It is absolute. And therefore, truth does not have sides to argue from.

> *Because beliefs are only relatively true, they aren't necessarily worth arguing over.*

A Reminder To Remember

People fight over conflicting beliefs, but never argue over the experience of absolute truth. So notice if you are ever trying to be right. It is a sure sign that you've temporarily left the peace of the real self and are in your mind thinking. The truth is there is only love. There is only this moment. There is only stillness. God doesn't make mistakes and nothing is ever wrong. But, hey, that's *my* truth. You are free to believe whatever you want.

The Peaceful Solution

Let go of needing people to agree with your opinions by experiencing truth yourself.

REASON #2 Being Liked

Be warned. It is a very risky strategy to let your peace be dependent upon whether or not people happen to like you. You have very little control over other people's opinions; and, unless the people in your life are aware of their own real self, they are going to base *your* likeability on *their* unclear mind conditioning. They are not going to see you clearly, but rather, only see their vastly edited, drastically distorted ideas about you – based upon their own prejudices and judgements.

> *Give yourself permission to relax. Let other people*
> *have whatever opinion they want. Focus on being*
> *present, peaceful, and loving.*

Being peacefully loving is the key that frees you from needing people to like you. It is so important because I've observed that 'living out of love' e.g., unaware of the source of love within you, is one of the main causes of physical conditions, emotional unease and life stresses.

Based upon hundreds of Mind Detox consultations, I've observed one core issue that sits at the heart of most people's problems. Namely, the belief, and subsequent distorted perception, that they are separate from the source of love and therefore have to *do* something to *be* lovable. This belief makes them work hard to 'get' love from others and, inevitably, end up disappointed. Not necessarily because other people don't love them, but because this outside love is never as intimate or fulfilling as the love found within a person's own heart.

A Reminder To Remember

Tremendous peace of mind is experienced when you can rest in the inner still silent source of love. If you ever find yourself needing other people to like you, it means that you've temporarily lost touch with your real self. The truth is you don't need anyone to love you because *you are love*. Play with this possibility. Notice what it's like not to look to others for reassurance or respect. Be self-sufficient. Free yourself from fears about what people might think about you. Discover that you don't need the external world to love you for you to be OK.

The Peaceful Solution

Let go of needing people to like you by resting in the inner still silent source of love.

REASON #3 **Problematic People**

Anger, hurt and sadness are common by-products of resisting the behaviours of others. For you to cultivate an ongoing experience of peace, it is vital that you let go of making other people behave how you think they should. Or at the very least, make your peace more important than them changing their ways. Otherwise your peace is going to fall victim to the uncontrollable actions of others.

> *"If it is peace you want, seek to change yourself.*
> *It is easier to protect your feet with slippers*
> *than to carpet the whole of the earth."*
>
> ANTHONY DE MELLO [5]

Peaceful people don't pin their hopes for peace on the actions of others. In his book *Awareness*, Anthony De Mello says, *"We are not here to change the world, we are here to love it"*. I love the power of this simple truth. In only a few words, he takes the focus away from us trying to change the external world and places the power and responsibility in our own laps; specifically, in our willingness to learn how to love fully. I would also suggest that we are not here to change other people, or make them behave as we believe they should. Rather, it is more useful to focus on learning how to love people as they are.

By love, I don't mean romantic love. Neither do I mean you have to agree with their actions. Love is unconditional, non-judgmental and allows people to walk their own path to peace.

A Reminder To Remember

If you ever have a problem with how a person is behaving, play with not letting their actions impact your peace. Compassion is a great way of doing this. A compassionate person knows there are no bad people and everyone is doing their best to experience peace of mind, love and happiness. If someone is acting in a way you don't agree with, then remember that they, like you, are doing their best. They don't know any better way, yet. Otherwise they would choose it. They need your compassion, not criticism.

The Peaceful Solution

Let go of people needing to behave how you think they should. Compassion sets you free.

REASON #4 Being On Time

Within the context of you experiencing your heart's greatest desire – peace of mind – being on time may seem very minor and unimportant. However, this is one of the most common reasons why people get stressed and forget to be peaceful.

A while back, I got caught in busy traffic on my way to deliver a talk on "Enjoying Peace of Mind". Although the traffic had stopped, the clock continued to tick and I was rapidly becoming late for my appointment. My mind automatically went into the future, started worrying about being late, and tension appeared within my body.

A Reminder To Remember

After a minute or so I suddenly became aware of the stress that was forming over my being late. I couldn't help but laugh out loud at how ironic it was that I was stressed over arriving on time to a talk on peace of mind! It became glaringly obvious to me, sitting in my car that day, that I was going to get to my appointment when I got there. Getting stressed wasn't going to get me there any quicker, and being caught in traffic was a chance to prioritize peace and enjoy the journey.

Incidentally, as 'luck' would have it, when I eventually did arrive at the venue for my talk, the fire alarm was ringing and everyone was waiting outside, not for me, but for the fire brigade. Although I was officially late, I was actually early!

The Peaceful Solution

Let go of needing to be anywhere faster than the time you arrive.

REASON #5 Fixed Future Plans

Focusing too much on the future is a very quick way to misplace your present peace. Having fixed future plans can also limit your life enjoyment. Fixed plans can cause you to become controlling and resist life if it doesn't happen the way you think it should.

However, what it is important to remember is that the future has a way of never working out exactly how you anticipated . So play with letting go of trying to make your life happen in any particular way. Much freedom comes from making your inner experience of life more important than your external life circumstances. That way you don't mistakenly wait until your life is exactly how you think it should be before you get to enjoy it.

A Reminder To Remember

Attachment to future plans happens when you need the future to make you happy, peaceful and loved. However, as you already know, all of these wonderful treasures can only be experienced right now. So if you ever notice your peace and happiness becoming dependent upon things changing, improving, or becoming better at some point in the future, then stop.

Make your inner subjective experience of life more important than your objective life circumstances. Fill your attention up with this moment. Make the most of this moment; and let this moment be enough. You will find that your attachment to future plans effortlessly falls away, to be replaced with peace. You will discover that when you are fully present you don't need the future to fulfil you; you are already full and complete as you are. Everything beyond this moment is merely a potential bonus.

The Peaceful Solution

Let go of needing your life to happen how you think it should. Let this moment be enough.

LET'S PLAY A GAME

Prioritizing Your Peace

Each day for the next five days, play with a peaceful solution and notice what happens to the levels of peace you experience:

- **DAY 1:** Let go of needing people to agree with your opinions by experiencing truth yourself.
- **DAY 2:** Let go of needing people to like you by resting in the inner still silent source of love.
- **DAY 3:** Let go of people needing to behave how you think they should.
- **DAY 4:** Let go of needing to be anywhere faster than the time you arrive.
- **DAY 5:** Let go of needing life to happen how you think it should. Let this moment be enough.
- Then on **DAY 6** consider this: What other things do I make more important than my peace? For the next two days, play with making your peace more important than the items on the above list.

The Eternal Game

This is genuinely going to be a game to play with… for ever! Prioritize your peace, playing with the techniques from Chapter 10 for thinking less and meditating every day to cultivate the habit of context awareness, or being aware of the still silent serenity of this moment. There is no end to the levels of peace, love and happiness you can experience.

Living Without Thinking In The Real World

When preferences and goals rise up, you effortlessly, and in a state of complete contentment, do whatever is required to make positive changes to your body or life. But because you are already perfectly peaceful, you are not attached to getting your preferences met or goals achieved. You are complete. Holding nothing you enjoy everything. You are surrendered to a wisdom that exists outside the parameters of your individual mind. Your attention is filled with love as you flow in the river of grace.

> *Resistance and therefore unhealthy stress is no longer chronic. Healing occurs organically, happiness flows naturally and peace is for life.*

Experiencing the world with awe-filled eyes, you welcome life however it may look and no longer resist life if it doesn't happen exactly as you think it should. Simultaneously, you experience no circumstances as bad and no emotions as negative. You have stepped beyond the dualistic mind-made illusion of separateness to rest in oneness and love.

But the best news of all is: *you can do it*. Peace is far easier than stress, resistance, pain and struggle. Give yourself permission to be at peace with your past by being present. Rest in your real self by noticing the presence of still silent peace within your awareness now, and play with taking life a little less seriously every day. You are walking the Path of Joy after all.

A Marvelous Way To Live

Making the shift from thinking about life to directly experiencing the fullness of life is the point of this book. Doing so is the magical key that opens the door of serenity within yourself and brings success in the wider world. It is a marvelous way to live. You experience yourself as a still silent peaceful presence of joy-filled love that is eternally present and absolutely infinite.

To think or not to think? The choice is yours.

*"The world
is built on magic,
not rocks."*

MSI [6]

Living Proof that Peace is Possible

• • • •

THE BIG BENEFITS FROM THINKING LESS

APPLYING THE LESSONS IN THIS BOOK CAN YIELD BIG BENEFITS.
Presented here are a handful of the many success stories from
people, like you, who have become fed up with thinking too much
and applied the principles in this book to enjoy more serenity and
success. There's no reason why you cannot expect the same results
if you apply these messages with your heart, mind, body and soul.
As you will learn, it is very much worth it.

Meet Jill, who had Debilitating Anxiety

I was getting daily bouts of anxiety, which were debilitating and
stopped me doing ordinary everyday things. I would shake, feel
sick, overeat to stop the nausea and rush about like a headless
chicken, not really getting anywhere. Since using the methods
taught by Sandy I have not had any anxiety, have much more
energy, been more focused and got more done.

My life has become calmer and happier, and consequently so
have the lives of those around me. I laugh a lot more and I'm sleeping better. Old behaviour patterns and past traumas are now a
thing of the past as I learn to live in and enjoy each moment.

Meet Jen, who was Tense all the Time

I was always worried that something bad was going to happen and anxious about what other people thought of me. It was a horrible strain on my body. I was totally tense and sometimes felt I couldn't breathe properly. I would get the shakes because I was so nervous and on edge. My neck and shoulders were in pain and I had even started going grey in my twenties due to stress.

Learning meditation with Sandy totally changed my perspective on life. I now see the world for the first time through awakened eyes. I've learnt how to take a step back from the commotion of my mind and to simply watch it. Making this shift helped me to realize that I am the peaceful awareness that is aware of my thoughts and emotions. What a relief. The real me is at peace and I didn't even know it! Thanks Sandy for helping me to meet my real self again, to stop worrying so much about what people think about me and to enjoy peace for life!

Meet Jemima, who had Panic Attacks

For years I struggled with panic attacks, constant anxiety and low self-esteem. But now, as I am writing this, I am filled with a sense of silent contentment. I am amazed that I am actually experiencing peace, happiness and joy! I feel as though I have found my real self and each minute I am falling more and more in love with who I am.

A little over eighteen months ago I learnt one of the simplest lessons of my life, a lesson that changed every aspect of my life in the most amazing ways. For decades, I lived my life in a state of fear, a state of stress and fatigue. Each day I worked to control my surroundings, thinking about every possible outcome of every action I made, fixing what I thought was broken and holding onto everything I had worked so hard to get – my friends, my job and my possessions. Unsurprisingly, all of this thinking and internal turmoil began to show up in my body, with chronic headaches, neck pain and consecutive injuries plaguing my days.

Over the course of a five-day retreat with Sandy all of that fell away, my addiction to over-thinking and controlling disappeared as I got to know an immense ocean of stillness, which existed within me. I learnt how to live in the present moment, no longer think about the future or try to change the past, and I was given the skills to be aware of inner stillness at any time no matter what the circumstances.

Every area of my life has been enhanced as my experience of the stillness deepens. My days now flow so smoothly and are filled with an incredible amount of peace, joy and happiness. I am no longer crippled by a sense of fear or anxiety, instead I am energized by an incredible excitement about the infinite possibilities each day holds and an immense gratitude for how simple it is to live a life of peace.

Meet Jenny, who wanted More from Life

I feel on top of the world, and knowing that I am perfect just as I am, right now, is just so liberating. I can't stop smiling. Thank you for sharing your peace and stillness with me and showing me a new way of being truly alive.

Meet Ivan, who was Stressed with Cancer

I learnt meditation with Sandy just a few weeks after being diagnosed with late-stage cancer. Without any doubt, I would not be alive today if it wasn't for this beautiful, simple and ancient form of meditation.

Although I was an expert at nutrition, exercise and coaching, I never knew how to effectively deal with stress. To be honest, I didn't even know I was stressed. I just automatically suppressed it. I had tried various systems of meditation and 'meditated' most days, because the scientific research was clear – meditation is very good for you. However, for me it was a chore, I found it difficult and didn't really feel much benefit and just figured it was because I wasn't good at it, or not suited to sitting still.

When I learned the meditation techniques that Sandy teaches at his Ascension Meditation course, I was shocked, by the dramatic effect it had almost instantly – I experienced, for the first time I could remember, pure peace! At the time I was in a great deal of consistent physical, mental and emotional discomfort, which had become my 'normal' experience of being alive, so the contrast for me was very clear. I even saw a physical difference in the inflammation in my body after just twenty minutes! Initially I didn't believe my own eyes, because nothing I had tried so far had helped! But it happened every time I practised the meditation. I continue to use the meditation today. It has given me access to really living a life full of joy, love and peace, no matter what the circumstance.

Meet Louise, who felt Stuck in Life

I became a wheelchair user in my mid 30s following a car accident that severely affected my mobility and left me in constant pain. I struggled on a day-to-day basis to look after my three sons and always felt inadequate. I didn't love myself, and couldn't see a way back to peace.

Through meditation I have, once more, discovered the joy in life. I realized that I was spending too long either depressed about the things I could no longer do or in a state of anxiety regarding my future. Regular meditation keeps me in the present and helps me to appreciate what I have right now. I have learnt to love myself and know that I am enough, just as I am. I may not have freedom within my body but meditation has given me freedom within my mind and it's beautiful.

Meet Robert, who had Clinical Depression

From the first time of meeting Sandy at a weekend workshop he transformed my life. From being a person who had lost the ability to smile, I came out on the Sunday with my jaws aching from smiling so much. I discovered peace in my mind and body. How did this change happen? It's very simple. I learnt how to let go!

I was on my third month of sick leave for clinical depression – low confidence, miserable and so very low. I was having terrible thoughts of ending my life – as I just could not get my mind in a good place. After spending one weekend with Sandy, it turned my whole outlook on life into a very happy and safe place. Sandy taught me how to use the methods and after only one day I could identify how easy it was to let go of negative thinking.

There are two very important memories I remember so vividly today, three years on... one that I couldn't stop smiling and two, the colours all around us are just so vibrant. Driving back from the course I could not stop noticing how beautiful the red colour was on the road signs! I have driven thousands of miles but honestly can say I have never noticed the red colour of the signs before! Secondly, I was met by my sister who said – "Look at you... you're smiling!" I use the meditation techniques everywhere and what a great feeling it is.

Meet Bianca, who wanted to End her Life

Going beyond my negative thinking has taught me how to live life with very little effort and to enjoy it. I can literally feel the warmth and energy circulate every square inch of my body. From wanting to end my life a few weeks ago, to discovering joy, freedom and peace – that's quite a result!

Meet Sue, who Worried Too Much

I've always appreciated nature but flowers seem more colourful and landscapes more awesome than ever before, even when I've seen them many times before – in fact most things seem more amazing. I meditate myself to sleep most nights and I've been sleeping much more soundly. I feel generally calmer and more accepting of whatever is happening even if it's something I don't like.

When I have down days there is a knowing that it won't last and it's OK to feel exactly as I feel – which brings a kind of peacefulness to me, even if I feel upset, angry or whatever. I now know I always have a choice when I notice my mind has taken over and I'm being "thunk" – which brings me a feeling of freedom that I didn't have before. I am even more understanding of others and much more accepting of exactly how they are or what they are doing. I am looking after myself better, which usually means I do less rather than frantically doing more and more to please others. I used to worry a lot about what others thought of me being so interested in healing and complementary therapies – believing they thought I was odd – but now I care a lot less about what people might think of me, which gives me the peace of mind to live how I want and be more open rather than hide away or do what I think is expected. This has led to feeling more confident and proud to be me. I also believe I have become a better therapist because of these changes in me.

Meet Sue, who was Postponing her Dreams

Prior to attending the meditation weekend course with Sandy I worked as a lecturer at a large health and beauty college, but had always dreamed of owning my own training academy. I was consumed by my fears of failing and not being good enough – which ultimately kept me firmly stuck where I was.

Meditating daily since the course has been effortless and I feel that I have found my missing peace. As a result, any fears I had linked with my dream of owning an academy dissolved too. Two years later I am now the proud founder and principal of a very successful training academy. Today many of my students have also learnt to meditate with Sandy, which enables them to lead richer and fuller lives.

Meet Gail, who was a Control Freak

After a weekend workshop with Sandy I really felt that I'd found the missing piece of the jigsaw in my life – an essential tool that could, at any time of day or night, bring me back to peace and calm, and more importantly, to the real me – my soul and connection to God.

I now use meditation to let go of thinking too much and connect with the infinite and abundant universal source of life. Everyone's experience of meditation will be different, but on a 'good' day, mine is like being picked up by a loved one when you were a little child and being given an enormous hug.

Meet Tina, who was Super-stressed

Driving home from the meditation course, I turned the radio off. This was a first for me as I always needed it to help quieten my mind. I meditated all the way home (with my eyes open of course!). I had never realized before that it was possible to meditate with my eyes open, just going about my daily life. The two-and-a-half-hour journey flew by and I arrived home feeling very calm, relaxed and uplifted.

I have meditated regularly for the last year and find that I need less sleep and actually feel more refreshed in the mornings. It has been a significant help during periods of high pressure at work, alerting me to the distracting chatter in my mind and enabling me to quieten these thoughts, so I can focus more clearly and calmly on the task at hand. I also regularly experience peace and contentment and would go so far as mentioning occasional feelings of bliss, which I find very strange to say, because I am usually quite emotionally and verbally understated. But I know it is true, because there is no other way of describing it. I know the peace is always inside of me and as time goes by I am able to choose to feel it more and more of the time.

Meet Lindsey, who was a Workshop Junkie

Being an absolute workshop junkie I had a library's worth of books about spirituality, magic, ancient practices, meditation and yoga and had even travelled to India in the hope I would find true peace and love there. Despite attending almost every workshop under the sun, I'd always been my own worst enemy and would often feel like a victim of other people's actions and behaviours, judging myself harshly within any situation or resisting life as it was.

Beginning to know myself through meditation has been such an empowering thing, allowing me to be brave, courageous and more honest than I would have previously dared. Knowing the still, silent space has given me a freedom within which I never dared to dream was possible for little old me. Previously I had been searching for love on the outside, looking for adulation and admiration from others. I've now discovered that love lives within me, waiting for me to simply notice it. I never thought it could be so simple. To not have to stop my mind like I'd tried to before, only to become aware of it and then let it be, to let go of having to control or figure life out. I've discovered all that remains is a gentle, underlying still silent peace-filled happiness that is pure magic, and still is to this day.

Life After Thinking Too Much

• • • •

YOU'RE GOING TO LOVE WHAT YOU CAN DO NEXT

CLUB: Join Sandy's online club where you can access videos, audios and articles as well as special offers.

CLINICS: Experience a private one-to-one consultation with Sandy or find a Mind Detox practitioner near you using Sandy's online practitioner finder.

COURSES: Learn more advanced forms of meditation with Sandy that are only ever taught in person.

RETREATS: Experience Sandy's unique mind–body–soul approach to health, peace and happiness at one of his residential retreats. Highly recommended!

ACADEMY: Make a positive difference to the lives of others by training with Sandy to become a qualified Mind Detox Method (MDM) practitioner.

For more info, visit: *www.sandynewbigging.com*

Acknowledgements

BIG THANKS to the Newbigging clan for always encouraging me to follow my heart. To Lindsey Dayavati Best for always being there for me. And to Micci Gorrod and Lee Johnson for creating such an inspiring environment for me to write.

I am grateful to the team at Findhorn Press including: Jacqui Lewis for editing the book, Richard Crookes for the brilliant cover design and Sabine Weeke for being a trusted sounding board through the entire project.

My heartfelt thanks also goes to every person who has attended my talks, clinics, academy courses and retreats. Without your courage to go for what you want this book would not have been possible. Finally, I'd like to thank MKI – your guidance has helped me to rediscover still silence – for which I am eternally grateful.

I also gratefully acknowledge all permissions given for the quotes used in this book, with particular thanks to MKI and Timothy Freke for their words.

1   from p. 56, *Awareness,* by Anthony de Mello © 1990 The Center for Spiritual Exchange. Published by Fount, reissue edition, 1997.

2   from p. 57, *The Buddha: Emptiness of the Heart,* by Bhagwan Shree Rajneesh (Osho) © 1989 OSHO International Foundation. With permission of OSHO International Foundation, www.OSHO.com.

3   from p. 5, *Awareness,* by Anthony de Mello © 1990 The Center for Spiritual Exchange. Published by Fount, reissue edition, 1997.

4   from *From Feeling Upset to Being Peace,* video talk by Eckhart Tolle © Eckhart Tolle. Published by www.eckharttolletv.com

5   from *Awareness,* by Anthony de Mello © 1990 The Center for Spiritual Exchange, 1990. Published by Fount, reissue edition, 1997.

6   from p. 108, *Ascension,* by MSI Maharishi Sadasiva Isham © 2010 Ishaya Foundation. Published by Ishaya Foundation Publishing Company.

About the Author

SANDY C. NEWBIGGING is the creator of the Mind Detox Method (MDM), Conscious Awareness Life Meditation (CALM), and author of several books including *New Beginnings*, *Life Detox*, *Life-Changing Weight Loss* and *Heal the Hidden Cause*. Sandy regularly blogs for the Huffington Post and contributes to Yoga magazine. His work has been seen on television worldwide on channels including Discovery Health. He has clinics in the UK, runs residential retreats internationally, and trains Mind Detox practitioners via his academy. For more information on talks or workshops given by Sandy C. Newbigging or to book him for a speaking event please use the following contact details:

answers@sandynewbigging.com
www.facebook.com/minddetoxman
www.twitter.com/minddetoxman
www.sandynewbigging.com

The Everyday Alchemist's Happiness Handbook
by Natalie Fee

"Happiness has been holding out its hand to you since the day you were born, longer perhaps, waiting for the time when you run out of excuses and say... yes." Packed with practical, down-to-earth advice, **The Everyday Alchemist's Happiness Handbook** *reveals how the choices we make on a daily basis affect our sense of fulfilment. It puts forward a set of highly accessible and effective tools to help each of us live brighter, happier lives.*

978-1-84409-587-2

FINDHORN PRESS

Life-Changing Books

For a complete catalogue,
please contact:

Findhorn Press Ltd
117-121 High Street,
Forres IV36 1AB,
Scotland, UK

t +44 (0)1309 690582
f +44 (0)131 777 2711
e info@findhornpress.com

or consult our catalogue online
(with secure order facility) on
www.findhornpress.com

For information on the Findhorn Foundation:
www.findhorn.org